Yaron Reshef / Out of the Shoebox

Yaron Reshef

OUT OF THE SHOEBOX

Copyright © 2014 by Yaron Reshef

reshef.book@gmail.com

Translated by: Nina R. Davis and Shira E. Davis
Cover design: Lee Oshrat

ISBN: 978-1502475565

Library of Congress Control Number: 2014917536

CreateSpace Independent Publishing Platform,
North Charleston, SC

This book is dedicated to the memory of: my father, whose image I succeeded in reviving through this book; my mother, who passed away while this book was being written; my father's friend Mordechai Liebman; my aunt Dr. Sima Finkelman; and the rest of my family members who perished in the Holocaust.

This book is dedicated to my family, so that they may pass the story on to future generations and keep these cherished memories alive.

Table of Contents

From Past to Present

I am certain that I never invited the past to walk into my life. Not that I didn't take an interest in our family's history. On the contrary – in my youth, as well as in later years, I did try to trace my family's roots and its history. Unlike my sister, who showed no interest in such matters, I eagerly absorbed any information relevant to my family. But no, I did not invite the ghosts of people long gone, nor the memories or emotions attached to them, to come visit me in Israel of 2012. It was as if some hidden hand orchestrated the perfect plot to pull me into the cauldron of family affairs.

It was as if this plot was produced especially in order to motivate me to embark on a year-and-a-half's worth of obsessive searching for long-lost details covered in the dust of history, memories erased by generations of silence. As if the invisible entity directing the action knew me intimately and knew full well that I could not rest when confronted with an open case, especially a mystery involving my relatives both near and far, and a considerable amount of money. So perhaps it was chance or fate that colluded to pull the strings of quite a number of people and circumstances, who jointly presented me with an impossible riddle. It was the ultimate tool to create an emotional trap that would not let me push the subject aside, not even for a single day.

If you were to ask me what would be the best way to evoke in me the strongest motivation to explore the saga of my parents' emigration to Israel and the fate of their families, I could not have come up with a more perfect puzzle; an attraction so aggressive in its pull as Life has presented me, in the form of a chain of chance events, during the past two years.

***

The Lot, Part I

I had no intention of writing a book. I had no need to write a story in general nor a story about my family and the Holocaust in particular. But life being what it is, sometimes things happen in mysterious, even surprising ways. Stuff that used to take center stage moves to the background, and background stuff moves downstage and center. That's what happened in my case.

I began putting things down in writing because people close to me – family, friends, colleagues – told me repeatedly that I simply must write the story of "finding the lot" – a plot of land purchased by my father in 1935 and discovered seventy-seven years later.

The story begins in early July 2011, while I was in the US for work. My wife, Raya, received an unexpected phone call. The caller wished to speak to Yaron, son of Shlomo Zvi Finkelman. The speaker was attorney-at-law Elinor Kroitoru, head of Location & Information at Hashava, The Company for Location and Restitution of Holocaust Victims' Assets. After introducing herself, Elinor asked Raya whether she had any information about a lot owned by my father in the country's north. Raya said that she knows my parents came from Poland, but knew nothing of a lot or any other property they may have owned there. Raya naturally assumed that Elinor's question had to do with property during the Holocaust, ergo in Poland, never suspecting that the lot in question was in Israel. At Raya's suggestion, Elinor contacted my sister Ilana, who said she knew nothing of a lot owned by my father in Israel. Elinor told her that her office had located a lot near Haifa, purchased in 1935 by one Shlomo Zvi Finkelman who lived in Haifa, and that she was trying to trace that person or his beneficiaries. Apparently, her office was quite surprised to find, among the lands purchased by Jews who perished in the Holocaust, one bought by a resident of Haifa. Elinor was asking for my father's address in 1935, hoping to connect between the buyer, whose address appears on the bill of sale, and our father. My sister replied that our father had lived at several addresses in Haifa after reaching Mandatory Palestine in 1932, among them Massada, Nordau, Hillel and Achad Ha'am streets. Elinor wanted to know the house numbers, of which my sister knew only two – 6 Nordau and 4 Achad Ha'am. Ilana suggested that as soon as I got back from the States I'd contact Elinor, because I may have further details.

A week later, when I got home, Raya told me about this unexpected phone call and how she had thought it was about a lot in Poland. "Talk to your sister," she urged, "she'll probably have much to tell you." Ilana mainly repeated the story, adding that, meanwhile, she received a letter from Elinor recommending that we contact the office of the Custodian General at the Ministry of Justice to find out whether we had a legal right to the property in question. "You need to find proof that the Shlomo Zvi Finkelman appearing in the bill of sale is indeed your father," said Elinor when I called her the next day. "I can't help you any further, it's out of my hands. But it would help considerably if you knew exactly where your father lived in 1935, who this Mordechai Liebman guy was, and what was his connection to your father." I was quite surprised at that, since I didn't understand how a Mordechai Liebman fit into the story.

My father died in 1958, when I was seven. Any memories I have of him are vague -- mostly a few images of going fishing together, when I joined him and his friends on the navy pier at Haifa Port. These pictures are engraved in my memory, thanks to the joint experience and because of a small but impressive number of fishing successes, attributed by my dad and his friends to beginners' luck. I also have some mental images of his work as a philatelist: hosting an American stamp merchant named Fogel in our living room, or sitting for hours sorting his stamps and trying to clean or fix damaged stamp perforations. I don't remember spending "quality time" with my dad, or any father-son talks. For all I know, I may have erased memories through years of suppression. His sudden death from a heart attack one winter night weighed heavily on me for years.

On the other hand, I knew quite a lot about him, because my "aunts" (all relatives other than the immediate family were typically called "aunt" and "uncle", as Polish Jews do), after the first affectionate cheek-pinching, would exclaim: "Gosh, the little one looks just like Junio!" My father, being the youngest child, was nicknamed Junio, probably the Polish version of Junior. Then they'd continue with tidbits of information about my dad's personality, or some other family-related lore.

I assume I collected these crumbs and stored them in my memory.

I suppose storing information in one's memory is easier than retrieving it when needed. But sometimes, when I have to recall things relating to my family history, I'm awed at the stuff that suddenly pops up, not quite sure whether these are true memories or the product of my imagination. Only after receiving proof or external corroboration am I convinced that it was true memory, actual knowledge. Therefore, I was not wholly surprised when I heard myself answering automatically: "Mordechai Liebman was a good friend of my father's in his home town, Chortkow; I think he perished in the Holocaust..."

"If you can find proof of that, it'll help when you have to provide the Custodian General with information and documentation," said Elinor.

So it came to pass that, in one day, my life took on a new focus: my father's lot, and with it the questions: Who is Mordechai Liebman? What was his connection to my father? What was his connection to the lot? And where did that kneejerk response to Elinor's question come from? I had some very vague childhood memories of tales of a lost lot, fragments of memories that must have come from two separate stories. The first was about a lot on Mt. Carmel that my father purchased. For some reason the name Shoshanat HaCarmel (literally "Rose of Carmel") stuck in my mind. The story was that my father bought the lot from a local crook who conned him, and my family never actually received ownership. The other lot-related story is even more complex. In my childhood, years after my father's death, while rummaging through forbidden cupboards, I came across drawings of what looked like an industrial building. Obviously, identifying it as an industrial structure came years later, when I learned to differentiate between types of buildings. To this day I clearly remember the drawing: flat, featureless façades, a perfect rectangular block with a saw-tooth roof; a sequence of right-angle triangles. Later, I learned at the Bezalel Academy of Arts & Design that this type of roof was very common in industrial and commercial buildings in the 1930s and '40s, meant to let in northern light while blocking direct sunlight. I vaguely remember a conversation with my mother, after she caught me snooping in the cupboard and looking at the drawings. "This was Daddy's dream," she said, "They wanted to build a kind of textile factory, similar to the ones in Poland... but it didn't work out because of the pogroms..." I recall that she referred to the location as Yishuv Haroshet (literally: industrial settlement) or Mif'al Haroshet (literally: industrial plant). "They bought the place from a rabbi who was a swindler who then disappeared." I know it sounds a bit strange that both snippets of memory have to do with lots and crooks, but my memory could have played tricks on me, mixing up the facts of the two tales. As for Mordechai Liebman, I knew nothing except that I once heard that he was a friend of my father's, or at least that's what I thought. Regarding my father's various addresses when he first came to Palestine, and my parents' later addresses as a married couple, I had only fragmented clues that did not add up to a clear picture. Though my mother was a hundred and one at this point, she hadn't been communicative for several years.

During the days that followed I began to get used to the idea that I was facing a new kind of challenge. According to Elinor's instructions, I was to formally apply to Ms. Hanni Amor, head of the National Unit for Location and Management of Property, at the Custodian General's Bureau of the Ministry of Justice, attaching Elinor's letter and asking them to handle the matter. And so I did: in mid-August 2011 I applied to receive ownership of a lot which, a month earlier, I didn't even know existed.

Smiling, Raya said decisively: "This is a message from your Dad." "Okay," I replied, "but why now? Don't you think it's just a tad late, after fifty four years?" This was no innocent message; it handed me quite a challenge seeking information when there's no longer anyone to consult or interview. That generation is long gone, and even my mother, alive at the time, was not fit to communicate and provide information. No way of knowing exactly what I was getting myself into...

I decided to phone Hanni Amor, and was surprised when she explained to me, politely and patiently, that she couldn't help me. "It is up to you to find proof that your father is the Shlomo Zvi Finkelman, who bought the lot. Unfortunately I cannot help you or give you any info about the lot and its location. You have to provide my office with proof of your father's residence in 1935 and his connection to Mordechai Liebman." By the end of that exchange I felt I'd reached a dead end. It seemed like a puzzle wherein I'm expected to join two pieces that didn't fit and place them precisely at an unknown address on an imaginary game board. Sounds surreal, right? That's just how it felt. For the first few days I was at a loss, had no idea where to begin. I searched for the smallest lead that would point me to the missing facts, but couldn't come up with any creative idea. I tried to put myself in my father's shoes, tried to imagine what he did upon arriving in Palestine, what trail he left which would help me track down his address. The second task was even more complex. Intuitively, I began with the basics: Who are you, Mordechai Liebman, and what was your connection to my father and the lot? Reason told me that Liebman's name appears on the bill of sale as my father's partner. I tried to visualize a situation wherein my father purchased the lot with a friend, perhaps to bring to life a shared dream, or simply in order to split the cost. This theory agreed with the facts as I knew them: My father first came to

Palestine in December 1932, then returned to Poland in July 1934 to marry my mother, Malia née Kramer, whom he brought back to Palestine with him three months later, in October of that year. Had my father gone abroad with the purchase documents and recruited his friend as co-buyer? I couldn't know for sure, but it sounded plausible. Or perhaps my father had made Liebman's acquaintance in Palestine, and they'd bought the lot together. But after careful consideration I discarded that possibility. Logic said that the only reason Hashava, the company engaged in locating Holocaust victims' assets, would contact me about the lot was if one of the lot owners had perished in the Holocaust. Since Father lived in Palestine during the years in question, and also died there, then obviously his partner – apparently Mordechai Liebman – died in the Holocaust. Based on this speculative premise, I embarked on my search for Mordechai Liebman. I began my quest with Yad Vashem archives. I searched for pages of testimony under the name Mordechai Liebman from Chortkow, my parents' home town in Poland, currently in the Ukraine. Nothing. I searched for testimonials about Holocaust victims from the Liebman family in Chortkow and found nine testimonials, none of which had any mention of Mordechai. Most of the testimonials were from the early '50s, and I assumed it would be impossible to locate the persons in question; the addresses were old, and the people probably long dead. Having found nothing in the Yad Vashem archives, I began searching the Internet.

My parents on board the Carnaro,
on their way to Palestine, 1934

No sooner had I typed into Google (in Hebrew) the key words Mordechai, Liebman, Chortkow, than I apparently found Mordechai, right there in the second link displayed, which was "Meiselman, Getter, Cheled, Arbel, David – Chortkow." That was a total surprise. I knew the Meiselmans, who later Hebraicized their name to Cheled. Asher Meiselman Cheled was a close friend of my parents'. As a child, after Father's death, I spent many school vacations at their place in Yad Eliyahu in south-Tel Aviv. Their younger daughter, Varda, was my age; she taught me to fly little kites made of paper and tied with thread. You could say it was similar to origami, long before that concept made it to Israel. Tel Avivians called this type of kite "kifka". In my home town of Haifa the kites were made of reeds and called by the name "tyara". Within minutes I realized that the web page I landed on was set up by Miri Gershoni, to commemorate the Jewish community of Chortkow.

The page showed family photos from Asher Meiselman's albums: his parents and his brother; my father as the head of Betar youth movement in Chortkow, surrounded by his girl troop who were members in the movement; and a photo of my parents and my sister Ilana, with Asher himself standing next to them in his British soldier's uniform.

But the real surprise was finding the photo of Mordechai Liebman. The bigger picture was beginning to emerge. They were friends, apparently; Betar troop members and my father their leader. I knew that my father was older than the Meiselman brothers: Asher was six years younger, Shmuel – five, and the other brothers even younger.

When I was a child Asher told me that, when my father left for Vienna to study architecture and building engineering, it was he – Asher – who replaced him as Betar leader. Though the photo of Mordechai next to my father and the Meiselman brothers attested to the latter's friendship, it was not sufficient proof of the connection between Mordechai and my father. I had to provide a document or some other evidence of their relationship. And so, unexpectedly, I had a photo of Mordechai from 1930, which I could look at to my heart's content, but I still couldn't talk to him, nor hear his version of the story of the lot.

So I continued to search memorial books and other Holocaust literature mentioning Chortkow, but in vain. No sign of Mordechai Liebman, save for the photo in my hand.

Mordechai Liebman, 1930

My father as Betar Leader in Chortkow, 1928

How am I to track down my father's address in 1935? Where did he live after his arrival in Palestine in December 1932?

I had no knowledge about his first years in the country, so had no choice but to write down all I knew from family stories I'd heard in childhood, and from my mother's memoirs as told to my sister and written down by her some 15 years ago.

My father's address appeared on the love letters he sent to my mother, from Haifa to Chortkow. In these letters he described his search for work and the tension between the different Zionist movements, and the way he, as a young revisionist in "red" Haifa, felt discriminated against. But most of all, these letters were full of love and longing, and plans for their joint future in their new homeland. These letters, which I'd read as a youngster, were eventually lost. I still remember them on the shelf next to the bed in my mother's bedroom, stashed in a carved wooden box made by my father, along with photos and postcards from family members who perished in the Holocaust. Years later, I arranged the photos in an album, but the letters themselves were gone.

Asher Meiselman, Ilana, my mother, and my father
Haifa, 1940

My mother said, in her memoirs:

"... Even before his return to Chortkow to marry me, my husband opened an office in Palestine with a partner. My husband was an architect while the partner, named Wolf, was an engineer. They had plenty of work, because Hadar Hacarmel neighborhood was being built at the time. There was a shortage of housing in Haifa back then...

We bought an apartment under construction on Hillel street in Haifa. It was a 2 bedroom apartment, one room of which was always rented out, because no one at the time enjoyed the luxury of two rooms.

We all lived modestly in those days. Until the building was complete, we lived at Uncle Herman's on Nordau street. That was a very difficult period for me, because Herman's wife, Heidi, was used to having maids and couldn't cook at all, while Herman loved such Jewish-Polish dishes as gefilte fish, stuffed cabbage, etc. So I was their unpaid cook (even though my family used to have a cook too, I had taken an interest and learned to cook.) Aunt Heidi started learning Hebrew, which she had been totally unfamiliar with. She spoke many languages: German, French, English; and decided to learn Hebrew. When half a year had gone by without her managing to grasp any Hebrew, she gave up, deciding it simply wasn't for her..."

According to my mother's memoirs, my parents' first apartment upon arriving in Palestine in 1934 was 6 Nordau St. I know that place well, having spent much time there in my childhood. The building was designed and built by my father for relatives who came from Austria. With its Bauhaus design, the building stood out. Most of the raw materials and interior finishes were imported from Europe, and the apartments were rented out on a monthly basis or for key-money, constituting a source of income for my relatives, who kept the property till their dying day. I therefore knew that during 1934 they lived at 6 Nordau, then moved to Hillel St., house number unknown. Father, who worked as an architect at the time with an engineer named Wolf, rented an office at 4 Achad Ha'am St. Later, my parents moved to that place, where my sister was born and where I was born in 1951. But as far as I know, they moved there only in 1937.

Having reached a dead end, I decided to try and contact Hanni Amor at the Custodian General's office, figuring that, at worst, she'd refuse to advise me on how to proceed. I explained that according to my mother's memoirs my parents lived first at 6 Nordau and then on Hillel St., number unknown. Hanni confirmed that the street where my father lived when purchasing the land was indeed Hillel rather than Nordau, but stressed that I need to provide the house number and some legal proof that the person who had lived there was indeed my father. She further repeated the requirement to prove the connection between my father and one Mordechai Liebman.

How on earth was I to find that elusive house number? Days went by, and no creative idea came to me. True, the task now boiled down to locating one certain building on one street, but said street had some seventy-five houses. I was at a loss. Based on my mother's memoirs, the move to Hillel St. occurred after a short period on Nordau. I knew that the house on Hillel was probably built in 1934, so that my parents must have moved in either late 1934 or early 1935. I had one more early memory, in which my mother described to me the switch from the comfortable life in Chortkow to the modest living in Palestine. She'd say: "At first I was a cook at Herman and Heidi's place, then we moved to Mayer Fellmann's place that was very small, and we always rented out a room to another lodger, and there was no privacy... everyone lived very modestly." This was my mother's way of saying that they lived in deprivation. Did my parents buy the apartment from this Mayer Fellmann? Was he the owner, or the contractor who built it? At the time, in the early 1930s, most housing in Hadar Hacarmel was built for home owners who also owned the land. These people financed the construction of the building, usually lived in one of the apartments and sold or rented out the rest. Mayer Fellmann may have been the proprietor from whom my parents bought their home on Hillel St. I decided that, if push came to shove, I'd scour City Hall archives for the building permits for all buildings on Hillel St., until I found one in the name of Mayer Fellmann. I knew the city's archives were computerized, which would make the task easier, but thought that, since I couldn't trust my memory regarding the landlord's exact name, I should postpone this hunt, which took on Sisyphean proportions.

Another possibility was that my parents had bought an apartment in one of the buildings designed by my father, who had designed several apartment buildings in Haifa, including the one at 6 Nordau, and another at 7 Bar Giora St. I began by looking into the ownership of the house on Bar Giora, in the hope that this would reveal the same landlord for both buildings, thus leading to the sought-after address of the flat on Hillel St. Imagine my disappointment when a search of the computerized city archives showed that my father's design, from early March 1936, was for a woman named Sara Chana Preminger – no connection to Mayer Fellmann nor to the address of a house on Hillel St.

I'd found out about the house at 7 Bar Giora St. thanks to an architecture student named Uri Zirlin, who'd studied at the Technion over fifteen years ago. Zirlin called my sister one day to ask if she was the daughter of Shlomo Zvi Finkelman, who was a Haifa architect in the first half of the 20th century. He recounted how, while writing a seminar paper for a course given by architect Silvina Sosnovsky and historian-cum-Israeli-architecture-researcher   Prof

Gilbert Herbert, he had to research a certain unnamed architect who'd designed a building on Geula St. in Haifa. The building assigned to Zirlin appeared in a study, commissioned by Haifa municipality, of conservation-worthy buildings. Zirlin was to locate information about the building's architect and try to find additional buildings designed by him in order to create a portfolio that would ultimately be part of the archives of the Technion's Department of Architecture. I thought that if I found this student's paper, I'd find additional facts about my father and other buildings he designed and built, and perhaps even hit on my objective, i.e. his places of residence in the '30s. I pondered the strange coincidence that Prof Herbert, my professor at Bezalel, gave a Technion student the assignment of researching architect Shlomo Zvi Finkelman and his contribution to architecture in Haifa, unaware that that the latter was my father.

Ilana prepared and sent Zirlin a summary of my father's biography that included: family background, architecture and engineering studies at Baugenwerbe Schule in Vienna, Austria; how he came to Palestine to study architecture at the Technion; info about several buildings he designed; how he worked as an architect for the British Mandate for two years during WWII; and later for the Israeli Ministry of Trade and Industry in Israel, when he worked on the planning and building of the Artists' Colony in Safed. Zirlin promised to send my sister a copy of his seminar paper, but failed to keep his promise.

I decided to try and find out whether Uri Zirlin's seminar paper was on record at the Technion, so that I could see what information about my father it contained. I knew that seminar papers were submitted during the fourth year of studies, so assuming the student had completed his studies, he might be working as an architect today. The next step was searching the Internet for "Uri Zirlin". There were several people by that name in Haifa, but none seemed to have any connection to architecture. Still, I thought it worthwhile to call four persons by that name living in the Haifa area. The first three proved to be irrelevant – "wrong number", "don't know any Uri Zirlin", but the fourth did indeed answer to that name. When asked if he by any chance knew an architect who'd studied at the Technion, he wanted to know why I was asking. I explained that I was looking for a person who'd written a paper about my father, and he replied that, though he'd studied architecture and worked at it for a while, he dropped this occupation. Moreover, he claimed he'd never heard of my father and never wrote a seminar paper about architectural conservation in Haifa. I detected a kind of evasiveness in his voice, so I apologized for the intrusion and hung up.

About architect Silvina Sosnovsky, on the other hand, I found plenty of material. Apparently she was very active as an architecture researcher in Haifa, who focused on the location and conservation of buildings built in the 1920s-1940s. When trying to find her via the Technion, I learned that she'd retired; and after explaining my reason for seeking her out, they agreed to give me her number so I could contact her directly. Ms. Sosnovsky graciously listened, took down my father's details and suggested I call her back a few days later. I waited in suspense for a week before calling again. "I remember your father's name," she said, "and I'm familiar with the buildings on Nordau and Bar Giora streets that you mentioned... they are indeed in a study of conservation-worthy buildings that I conducted for the City of Haifa in 2001... but I can't find any other material related to him... Nor can I find any mention of your father in my other published work... I'd advise you to apply to the Technion's Architectural Heritage Research Center... Maybe there's documentation of your father's work there, as well as copies of papers written by students whom I supervised."

What a let-down. I expected to garner some sort of new information, or a clue at the very least. But my high hopes were dashed. The very next day I tried to contact the Research Center, but though I found information on its activities on the Internet, it took a whole week of persistent attempts until I finally got through to them on the phone. The woman at the other end of the line, Hedva, listened patiently to my story, took down some notes, asked me to email her a few more details about my father, and said she'd search the archives, warning me that it would take time. "However," she added, "if there is information about your father, it will turn up." Two weeks later, after intensive searching, nothing turned up. Apparently there was nothing about him in the archives.

As I was dialing Hedva's number to thank her for her efforts, it occurred to me that I hadn't mentioned that my father had been a Technion student for about two years before embarking on an architect's career in Haifa. "Then why don't you try to find out whether your father's student file still exists in the archives," Hedva suggested when I told her. Does the fact that my father was a student there change anything in the way her search was conducted? I wondered; it had never occurred to me. I did not for one minute expect his student file to still be there, after seventy eight years. But, figuring I had nothing to lose, I proceeded that very day to call the office of the Technion's graduate program in architecture to ask if there's any chance of finding any record or information relating to my father. I spoke to Ms. Ada Sales, graduate studies coordinator. "Look," she said, "there's not much chance that we'll find anything relevant, so don't expect too much. Many files were damaged over time. But if it's there, it will be found." She asked me to send her a copy of a will or any other document proving that I'm my father's beneficiary, to ensure I had the right to any information, should it be found.

I immediately wrote to Ada:

"Dear Ada, thank you for your time and your willingness to help. I am seeking information related to my father's studies at the Technion's Department of Architecture, his student registration file or any other relevant information. My father studied at the Technion in the early 1930s, between 1932-1935 I believe. His name was Salmon Hirsh Finkelman, though he Hebraicized his given names to Shlomo Zvi, and appears in some documents as Shlomo

Hirsh Finkelman. My father died in 1958 when I was seven, so I don't have much to go on. I'm particularly interested in finding out facts about the period of his life before he married and started a family. At your request, I'm attaching a copy of the probate which states the date of his death and the fact that I am his son and one of his beneficiaries. In that document, my name appears as Yaron Menachem Finkelman. I later Hebraicized my surname to Reshef. I am also attaching photos of my father's first British ID, but I think it was issued a few years after his Technion days. My father arrived in Palestine on a student visa, without an ID. I can be reached by email or phone, see contact details below. Thank you in advance and have a good day, Yaron."

Nine days later, while I was in the States on business, I received Ada's reply:

"Hi, I've retrieved from the archives a few files that seemed to me similar to the information you supplied, and have them handy. You're welcome to come over and peruse the material. All the best, Ada."

I replied at record speed. I told her I was in the US for two weeks, and asked if I could call her for more details. Ada replied within minutes with a phone number, which I called immediately, very excited. It was enough for me to hear a few details about the retrieved files to realize that one of them was my father's enrollment record. "There's only one problem," said Ada, "contrary to what you said, your father didn't actually study at the Technion at all. He did apply and was accepted, but the file contains no record of actual studies." Ada continued to explain that the enrollment file contains several letters in my father's handwriting, and invited me to come and see the material. "Maybe we'll be able to give you the entire file, and keep copies for us... Your father's penmanship is beautiful and his Hebrew is excellent. His entire file is preserved in perfect condition."

I can't begin to describe my excitement. I'd finally found a lead connected to my father. I began imagining what might be in the file, shook up by the revelation that my father apparently did not study in the Technion at all. My time in the US stretched out infuriatingly slowly, as I counted the days till my return. Gradually it began to sink in that the Technion's information would probably not shed any light on my father's place of residence. If he never actually studied there, what were the chances that his student record contained his address in Palestine? On the other hand, I hoped the file would contain the address of my father and his family in Chortkow – something I lacked and would be thrilled to acquire.

As soon as I got back I called Ada and made an appointment for the following day. I didn't know what to expect, couldn't imagine what I'd soon see.

The trip to Haifa flew by... Ada pulled out a gray folder containing an assortment of letters and documents. I immediately recognized my father's handwriting, with which I was familiar from old documents found at my mother's many years earlier. His handwriting was legible and the style clear and fluent, as if written in the writer's mother tongue. The folder contained correspondence between a young man applying to study architecture and construction and an academic institution detailing the admission requirements.

This is my father's first letter to the Technion:

Chortkow, 8 Aug 1932
To: The Office of the Registrar, the Technion, Haifa

a) I am writing to you with a request that you send me all information relating to admission to the Technion. I myself graduated from the construction school Baugenwerbe Schule Wien in Vienna. I studied for three years (six semesters) and have practiced for three years. Therefore I would like to know which year I can be accepted into.

b) I would also like to ask you to give me information on how I can immigrate to the country. If you can send me a demand, if you have one. And what guarantee is required.

I kindly request that you reply as soon as possible, so that I can forthwith follow my desire to study in a Hebrew Technion.

With best wishes and shalom,

S. Zvi Finkelman

My address:

Salmon Hersz Finkelman

Czortkow
279 Szpitalna .nl
Polania

I could tell immediately that my father went through the motions of applying to the Technion not because he truly wanted to study there, but with the intent of emigrating to Palestine, using studies at the Technion as a means to that end. The fact that my father refers to his studies of architecture in Vienna as though it was merely secondary school seemed a way to make double-sure that he'd be accepted. Anyone who looked carefully at the diplomas my father attached could easily see that he'd attended an ordinary high school in Chortkow – referred to at the time as a gymnasium – then continued to study architecture in Vienna. Though my father sent the original diplomas from the Vienna institution of higher education, it seems that no one looked into them too closely, accepting my father's statements at face value. According to my father's letter to the Technion, he studied six years in high-school plus another three years at a high-school for architecture in Vienna – a total of nine years, which is highly unlikely.

My father was accepted into the first year. He did not dispute this decision, only urged the Technion to send him a letter of admission. The Technion sent a copy of the admission letter to the British Mandate authorities, which in turn granted my father the sought-after entrance permit to Palestine. The letters were arranged chronologically in the folder: a letter from my father followed by the Technion's reply, and so on, as if time stood still. It was easy to see that a letter between Haifa and Chortkow took about two weeks. I must say that the Technion had been amazingly efficient in its replies, generally answering on the following day. My father, who wished to make aliya (immigrate to Israel) as soon as possible, continued urging the Technion, saying he was very eager to begin his studies in early 1933.

As strange as it may sound, I was somewhat disappointed. Though I knew by now I would not find Father's first Haifa address in this folder, I continued to pore over the folder with Ada, reading one letter after another and joking about my father's assertive way of pressing the Technion to speed up his acceptance. Later, when I continued to explore where Father got the idea of trying for a student visa, it turned out that Zionist activist Ze'ev Jabotinsky visited Chortkow in 1930 – the same year Father returned from Vienna and was appointed leader of Betar in his hometown, where the movement had some 150 members. In his talks, Jabotinsky used to enumerate the different ways of immigrating to Palestine, including student visas. Only in late February 1932 did Jabotinsky publish his article On Adventure, in which he called for illegal aliya to Eretz Israel. I have no doubt that my father was influenced by these ideas. Ada and I continued perusing page after page, admiring the correspondence. Once my father sent his transcripts, the Technion's reply arrived on 28 Sept 1932, saying that my father was accepted into the program, but had to immediately send the deposit of

15 Israeli lira   plus 500 mil for the visa expenses. Their letter stresses: "After the visa process which takes a few weeks, we must point out that if your trip is delayed so that you arrive here after Jan 1st, 1933 you will not be able to begin studying this school year." It took the letter a week to reach my father, but he could not buy Israeli lira in Chortkow. He bought American dollars instead, sending the cash with the following letter:

Chortkow, 11 Oct 1932

To: The Hebrew Technion, Haifa

Enclosed is the sum of IL 15 + 500 Israeli mil, guarantee and expenses as requested. It is impossible to get liras here so I am forced to send dollars at today's [exchange] rate of $3.46 . I shall gladly reimburse you for any unforeseen expenses upon my arrival.

Kindly expedite the issuance of my visa, so that I don't miss the 1.1.1933 deadline and don't miss a year's study.

Kindly confirm receipt of the money.

My name: Salmon Hersz Finkelman

Born: 24 March 1908

Parents' names: Izak Finkelman, Ryfka Finkelman, Drucker

Enclosed are a personal certificate and $54

With greetings to Zion S.Z. Finkelman

Father's letter with the cash got delayed in the mail, and on Oct 10, 1932 the Technion wrote: "This is to inform you that your letter of acceptance as a student has already been mailed. Since to date we have not received the deposit, we could not submit your papers for a visa and you will therefore not be able to study in the academic year 1932/33. As for your intent to come to Israel as a tourist, we cannot advise you." I can just imagine what went through my father's mind at the receipt of this letter. The drama at his home must have continued for about a week until, 8 days later, another letter from the Technion arrived, confirming receipt of the money. Nonetheless, the Technion reiterates that time is short, and my father may not be able to start his studies as planned and may have to postpone his arrival by a year. That same day, Oct 28, 1932, the director of the Technion wrote to the British Mandate's head of the Department of Immigration & Travel in Haifa, with an urgent request to issue a student visa for my father.

A month later the longed-for visa confirmation reached the Technion, which in turn gave my father the good news by registered mail: "We hereby send you a certificate with which you can receive the visa to Palestine from the British Consul in Warsaw. Please inform us directly when you expect to leave, so that we may determine whether you'll be able to begin your studies this year or only in 1933-34.

My father arrived in Haifa on Dec 26th 1932, and the next morning presented himself at the Technion and signed all enrollment and declaration forms required by the British Mandate authorities. He completed his mission in time: immigrated legally in 1932, five days before the year's end.

Ada gave me my father's file, comprising all of two sheets of cardboard. One had my father's personal details, and the list of subjects and grades for the four years of study.

Clearly, nothing was ever entered on this page. Which – as Ada pointed out – indicated he never studied after being accepted. The other sheet showed the tuition and payments made, and is proof that my father made the first three payments, totaling 12 lira and 300 mil of the IL18 he was to pay for the first year. In other words, my father indeed did not study at the Technion, but used his enrollment as a legal way to make aliya.

The declaration my father signed at the Technion on 27 December 1932:

Declaration

I, Shlomo Zvi Finkelman, upon receiving permission to enter the country as a student of the Hebrew Technion in Haifa, herewith deposit with the Hebrew Technion in Haifa the sum of fifteen lira as guarantee that should I wish to leave the country within four years of my arrival, I shall do so immediately at my own expense; otherwise the Hebrew Technion in Haifa shall be permitted to use the sum of 15 lira towards the expense of returning me to my country of origin. In such a case the Technion will not have to account for its expenses for my return, based on the permission hereby given to it.

In addition, I agree to leave Israel as soon as I remain without funds or should I become a burden to the public during those four years, and in case I fail to do so I agree that the Hebrew Technion of Haifa shall make all arrangements it deems fit to return me forthwith to my country of origin.

Signed: _____ [S. Zvi Finkelman]
Haifa, 27/12/32
Witness _____

Address: The Technion Business or Position

Witness: _____
Address: _____ Business or Position

There was one more envelope left. With two letters inside. An accompanying note and a declaration the Technion demanded. For some reason my father had forgotten to mail it together with the deposit. When he realized, thirteen days later, he hastened to mail the declaration with the following note:

"I attach the declaration which I forgot to mail previously. Please be informed that all my papers are now in order. Kindly try to send me the visa as soon as possible so that I may come before 1.1.1933. I remain, respectfully, S.Z. Finkelman."

I carefully detached the declaration from the top page, looked at it, and must have gone pale. Ada asked me with concern: "What's wrong? What did you see?" My expression must have given me away. It took a few moments before I got my breathing under control. "Mordechai Liebman and Shmuel Meiselman signed this page," I mumbled. "I don't understand," she replied, "Who's Mordechai Liebman? Who's Shmuel Meiselman?" "Don't you see? I was looking for my father's address in Haifa, and found proof that Mordechai Liebman was his friend." Ada looked at me, still confused. "I'll explain. I know it sounds strange and maybe illogical, but I found what I was looking for. Weird thing is, I wasn't even looking here for proof of a connection between Mordechai and my father. There was no logical reason to look here. You know, when I came to see the documents you found, I prayed that they'd contain info on my father's places of residence. Only here did I find out that he never studied at the Technion, which is why there was no address on record.   But I did find his parents' address in Chortkow; and even more significant was the discovery of proof that Mordechai Liebman was a close friend, since he wouldn't have signed that declaration otherwise."

This was probably the last testimony a man named Mordechai Liebman left, before being murdered in the Holocaust. There isn't even a testimonial page for him at Yad Vashem; but here he exists. After calming down, I gave Ada a brief version of the story of the lot and the partnership between my father and Mordechai Liebman.

Stranger yet was the fact that the Technion apparently had no need for that declaration and didn't use it, which is why they didn't bother informing my father that he hadn't mailed it. Only when Father finally came to the Technion was he required to sign the original declaration. The enrollment forms must have mentioned that he would be required to sign such a statement, and in his eagerness my father construed that to mean that it must be done immediately.

Thanks to that mistake I found proof of the connection between my father and Mordechai. The second witness, Shmuel Meiselman, brother of Asher Meiselman, was Father's friend from Betar – which I knew about. The connection between the three – Mordechai, Shmuel, and Shlomo Zvi – explained Mordechai's photo appearing on the Meiselman family memorial page on the Chortkow website. I felt that the pieces of the puzzle were beginning to fall into place.

I came back from the Technion holding a treasure; I'd received the folder with my father's original documents.

It was an amazing feeling. As soon as I reached the office I showed my partners the letters, so proud of my dad's beautiful Hebrew and penmanship. You couldn't tell from his handwriting that Hebrew wasn't his mother tongue; it looked well practiced, without any corrections or erasures. The writing, done with a fountain pen, was fluent, without those typical dots which occur when a fountain-pen user stops or hesitates.

With immense pride I showed my partners the school transcripts, as if the grades on those Vienna documents were my own, and the stylized handwriting was mine.

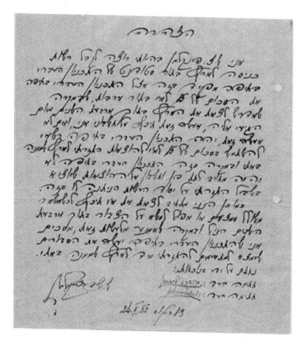

The declaration with the signature of witnesses Mordechai Liebman and Shmuel Meiselman

Declaration

I, S. Z. Finkelman, wish to gain permission to enter the country as a student of the Hebrew Technion in Haifa, herewith deposit with the Hebrew Technion in Haifa the sum of fifteen IL   as guarantee that should I wish to leave the country within four years of my arrival, I shall do so immediately at my own expense; otherwise the Hebrew Technion in Haifa shall be permitted to use the sum of 15 lira towards the expense of returning me to my country of origin. In such a case the Technion will not have to account for its expenses for my return, based on the permission hereby given to it.

In addition, I agree to leave Israel as soon as I remain without funds or should I become a burden to the public during those four years, and in case I fail to do so I agree that the Hebrew Technion of Haifa shall make all arrangements it deems necessary to return me forthwith to my country of origin.

Signed by me in the presence of:

Witness signature: (-) [Mordechai Liebman]

Witness signature: (-) [Shmuel Meiselman]

(-) S.Z. Finkelman

Chortkow, 24/X/32

"You've got to write this story... this is an unusual development and this is only the beginning," said

Hanan, my partner. "There's potential here for a fascinating story."

"I'm not sure it's of interest to anyone but me, but I'll think about it," I answered out of politeness, but I actually smiled to myself; the idea appealed to me. All that's needed is for events to continue to unfold, so as to add volume to the story, I thought to myself, as I continued to elaborate on the fantasy.

That week I asked my sister to do a thorough search at her home to see if she could find any other letters or documents relating to our parents that could shed light on their early years in Palestine. She didn't come up with anything new, but gave me the few documents she did have, including our mother's memoirs written over 15 years before I embarked on this quest.

It happened one Saturday morning, around 5:30 a.m. I woke up with a start, soaked in sweat, both body and sheets. For a moment I thought I must've peed in my sleep, but within seconds it all came back to me with incredible clarity: my father appeared to me in my dream. I can't help chuckling as I write, the last sentence sounds to me like something out of a folk tale. But I actually did dream about my father. I dreamed that I was lying in bed, and Father suddenly appeared. He stood by my bed, looking at me from above. He looked far younger than I remembered him – perhaps 35 or 40. A little like the photos in the family album I made many years ago, from the photos my mom had kept. I'd gotten used to the fact that Father kept looking younger over the years, particularly in the picture my mother had framed after his sudden death; a picture that hung on the wall over her bed all those years. As time went by and I got older, he became younger, like the picture of Dorian Gray. He stood there and looked at me, and at Raya sleeping next to me, for a few moments. Then suddenly, before I even uttered a word, he took out a gray cardboard folder that contained architectural drafts and drawings, and began telling me about the design of the building: "See, we wanted to build an industrial plant. The structure was very simple, no decorative features. The main thing in the design was the north-facing windows. They gave the building its unique character. Like a box with saw-teeth over it. The windows were on the roof, you know – to let northern light into the building. Light rather than sun. Here in Israel the sun is very strong, too blinding; not like the soft sun in Europe. The windows were like a series of triangles on the roof; the triangle's slope facing south, its vertical side facing north, repeated thirty times. The vertical side is glass and the slope is metal. That was the way to catch the light but not the sun. Direct sun is from the east and west; from the north we only get light. But you already know that we never built it – it didn't work out. The lot remained empty all these years, nothing was ever built on it."

The drawings and sketches were clear and sharp, the way I remembered them from childhood. There was no doubt that I'd seen them in the far past. They looked nothing like modern architectural drawings. There were no trees, people or cars. You could only figure out the scale based on the size of the windows in the roof and the height of the doors at the front. The proportions were pleasing and the structure looked aesthetic despite its simplicity.

Father's voice was faint but very clear, as if he was ensuring that I understood every detail. "Don't be surprised, that was my name: Salmon Hirsh Finkelman. That's the name on official papers. But on drawings and plans I was always Shlomo Zvi Finkelman. That was my Israeli name, my name as an architect, my new name. I wanted to leave the old name behind."

Suddenly Father's voice changed, became much louder, sounding like a reprimand. And indeed, he was scolding me: "I don't understand how come all these years you neglected the money in the bank.

You're irresponsible! It's unacceptable for the money to lie in the account unused, losing its value, and you people don't care. Find it and take care of it." Father's voice continued to intensify, turning into unpleasant yelling, scolding me... and that's when I woke up with a start, drenched in sweat. I lay in bed, trying to get my breathing back to normal. My heart was beating fast and loud, an unpleasant buzzing sound in my ears. I was panicking. For fifty-four years I hadn't dreamt of my father. Not one dream. Some years I prayed that he'd appear to me in a dream, but it never happened. As a child I believed that if I succeeded in holding my breath for a very long time, he'd appear. I have no idea where I got that notion, but obviously it didn't work. The only thing I got from those attempts were severe headaches. In this dream-state encounter we did not share a conversation. It was Father's monologue. A monologue starting with a pleasant explanation and ending in a scolding.

After my breathing returned to normal, the pounding of my heart and the buzzing in my ears calmed down, I quickly showered, while Raya slept soundly on, unaware of my distressing experience. I barely dried myself. Half-wet, I just grabbed a pair of shorts and the first available T-shirt from the wardrobe and put them on, quietly left the bedroom and went downstairs to the kitchen. I filled a tall glass with water and ice and gulped it down in an unsuccessful attempt to fight the dryness of my mouth and quench my thirst. I downed one glass after the other until my thirst and agitation abated. I acted automatically, without thinking or planning. Took out my laptop from its case, plugged it in, and while it was booting I smiled, thinking to myself: "I'm a good boy; I'm going to do exactly what Slomon Hirsh Finkelman asked me to do: find the money." For the first time in my life I typed into Google the words "Salomon Hirsh Finkelman" (I actually made the mistake of writing Salomon instead of Salmon.) Many times in the past I'd conducted web searches of my father, but never using his European name. This was the first time, just as Father commanded in my dream. The search results loaded promptly. I was flabbergasted. At the top of the page, the very first result was a link to a Bank Leumi web page with the names of unclaimed funds: "Unclaimed Accounts and Safes". I gasped. Still in a daze, for one moment I doubted that I'd really seen my father's name in the search results, but within a split-second I was sure. I clicked the link and a web page opened to an alphabetical list of surnames beginning with the Hebrew letter peh (as in Finkelman). And there it was, in the center of the page: Hirsh Salmon Finkelman and Mali 35.92 lira.

Father's name, and the first letters of Mother's name, Malia. Details serving as proof that I found the money, all within less than half an hour of waking up from the dream. I thought it strange that my father was the only one on that list of people with lost assets whose first names appeared before the last name, as if he wanted to make a point: I was here. Or maybe it was a message from an alternate reality. I have no problem accepting complex or weird dreams; but dreams that become reality within minutes are a bit difficult to digest.

Google Results page, in Hebrew.
My father's name is marked

It's hard to make sense of how, after fifty-four quiet years, a stream of events related to Father suddenly occurs, with each carrying a kind of gift: an unknown lot, a small sum of money in a forsaken bank account; and – possibly most significant to me – the rare chance to peek into faraway lives about which I knew so little.

By now it was seven a.m. I went back to the bedroom, changed into gym clothes and drove to my usual gym in nearby Pardessiya. I simply had to be physically active to get myself back to the present, and to my present-day self. Raya slept on serenely, as if nothing had taken place right next to her.

Time at the gym flew by. An hour's hard training passed, but I couldn't let go of recent events. Why now? Why does the story of Father's lot suddenly pop up, after seventy years? Why do I suddenly dream of Father, after fifty years, then within minutes find a forgotten bank account? Is Father pulling the strings, from another dimension? Have I been summoning these events with my thoughts, inviting them into existence? I had no answers. Not for a moment did I believe that something in my actions could bring about the weird, fascinating events that I have been experiencing. My general emotion was happiness; I was taking part in an amazing string of events; though I was somewhat bothered by the feeling of not being in control of the plot. I felt like an actor in someone else's play.

Raya listened to the story. When I pulled out the printed web page proving the existence of Father's bank account, I saw the doubtful expression leave her face. "He's continuing to send you gifts," she said with a smile. "Strange, after so many years... or maybe it just takes the mail a long time to get here..." "Or maybe he's just far away," I replied cynically. No doubt about it – once the initial shock wore off, I was left with a good feeling. I felt Father by my side.

I waited impatiently for the new week to begin. I wanted to call Hanni Amor and tell her that I had a document signed by my father and Mordechai Liebman that attested like a thousand witnesses to their connection. On that day for the first time I felt a new need: to try and investigate, to look back and know more about my family. The story about the lot was important, but I felt that the message delivered was: "There's a story of a family, an era, that's been waiting for years to be told."

A new week began. "That's an amazing story!" was Hanan's reaction when I told him the weekend's events. "I hope you're writing it all down... this is a story that must be told." This time, his words seemed to echo those reverberating in my own head.

I called Hanni Amor at the Custodian General's office, and told her excitedly about my visit to the Technion that resulted in my having an original document attesting to the connection between my father and Mordechai Liebman, "both signed on the same document... I found a document that had been waiting for me seventy-eight years." The voice at the other end of the line showed no emotion. "Did you find his address?" No, I did not. That was the goal of the search at the Technion, but – as sometimes happens – I looked for one thing and found another. I'd found at least 50% of what I was looking for, and I thought that was the hardest part... Truth is, I was sure I wouldn't find proof of a connection between the two men, but to my surprise that was precisely what I found. Still, it wasn't enough. I had no idea how to continue searching. It seemed that the only thing left to do was review all the building permits for all houses on Hillel St. and find the name of the owner of the lot on which the house where my parents lived in 1935 was built. I had a vague memory that the lot owner's name was Mayer Fellmann. This type of search was a desperate, time consuming act, but if I had no other choice, I'd do it. It meant 75 residential buildings, but it was doable.

Hanni listened patiently, then advised: "Try the Haifa City Archives, maybe your father's name and address are on file there... I need for you to find his address and bring me proof." I felt this wasn't fair. In my opinion, the document I found showed unequivocally that my father was the same Shlomo Zvi Finkelman who'd bought the lot together with Mordechai Liebman. What are the chances that another man by the same name lived in Haifa in 1935 and was Mordechai's partner in buying that lot? I was determined to continue looking and find my parents' address. "Okay," I conceded, "I'll start searching the archives." "Good luck," said Hanni.

By the end of November, after I'd despaired of finding new info, I called Haifa City Archives and told them I needed to find my parents' address in Haifa in 1935. "It's a waste of time," a librarian named Luba replied. "The records from that period won't do you any good. The only archived item that has the names of Haifa residents' addresses is the Electoral Register, but the records for those years are arranged neither by address nor by surname, it would take you ages to search through them for your parents' names, and most likely you won't find anything. I'll try to order from the archives whatever we have, and we'll contact you when the material gets here."

I was surprised to get a call from the Archives manager only three days later. To my chagrin, she said they didn't have anything from 1935; they only had a registry of voters from 1939. "Sorry," I said, "that wouldn't do me any good because I know for a fact that at that time my parents lived at a different address – 4 Achad Ha'am."

Still, I did not give up. I was sure that somewhere there must be documents or other evidence that showed where my parents lived. I began obsessively searching the web, trying to find ways of locating people's addresses seventy years back. Though I knew rationally that it may be impossible, I couldn't accept that thought, couldn't give in and give up. I looked for clues to the existence of resident records, phone books, addresses from that period, but came up empty-handed. After a week of endless searching I came across an article about archives with historical information from before the establishment of the State of Israel (i.e., pre-1948), and thus Iearned about the Zionist Archives in Jerusalem. After a brief phone call, I decided to write to the email address on the Archives home page: "... I am searching for my father's address: Shlomo Zvi Finkelman (Salmon Hirsh Finkelman) in the years 1933-1935. I know he lived on Hillel St in Haifa, but need to find the house number. For a while, at that address my mother Malca (Malia) Finkelman and my aunt Dr. Sima Finkelman also resided ... Please help me find whether there is any relevant info in Haifa's Electoral Register for 1933-1936; do you have these records in your Archives and do they contain exact addresses... Also, are there any other sources of information where I might find addresses where he lived during those years."

The first, encouraging, reply arrived within days: "A preliminary inspection shows we have two folders containing the Electoral Register in Haifa for the years 1935-1936. The folder numbers are J1/6670/1-J1/6670/2. To look at them you'd have to come to the Archives and request for them to be made available in the Reading Room. Kindly phone to schedule your visit."

So, first, I learned about the Electoral Register in Haifa. It was a book of all Jewish residents of Haifa, published by the Haifa Hebrew Community Committee in 1936. I learned that the census, conducted by calling on residents' at their homes, was aimed at proving that there were more Jewish than Arab residents in Haifa.

I called to schedule an appointment. The woman I spoke with said that, as far as she knew, there was an identical set of books in the Tel Aviv City

Archives. "Surely you mean Haifa?" I asked. "No, I mean Tel Aviv... they have a large, well organized archive, and if they have it, they'll be happy to help you, and you won't have to schlep to Jerusalem."

I called the Tel Aviv City Archives and briefly explained to a polite woman named Nelly what I was looking for. "We do have what you need: we have several phone books from that period, plus a copy of the book of Jewish residents of Haifa, published by the Haifa Hebrew Community Committee in 1936, the same book as in the Zionist Archives in Jerusalem. As for the information, you'll have to come here and look. The material is neatly organized, you won't have any trouble." I felt I was nearing my goal, though not at all sure I'd find relevant data about my parents; I didn't think my father had a phone in his office. He certainly didn't have one at home, because I clearly remember getting our first phone in 1963. As for the census, I fervently hoped that my parents were at home when the census-takers came knocking. I made the appointment at the Archives for the nearest possible date, January 22, 2012.

I had about a week and a half before my visit at the Tel Aviv Archives. Since I couldn't stand the tension of just waiting for the time to go by, I decided to take a chance on a few houses on Hillel St. and check on the Haifa City website, with its computerized database, whether one of them had a building permit in the name of Mayer Fellmann. Let's see, I thought, what would be faster: my random attempt to find info or the Tel Aviv Archives. Amused by the idea, I began my search: Number 7, Hillel – permit issued to Hanan Contractors in 1947. Ergo, irrelevant. No. 4, Hillel – permit issued to Ahuzat Yesha Co. in 1948. Clearly these buildings were built later. Maybe I should try further up the road. No. 10, Hillel – permit issued in 1947 to one Jaeger Engelrod. Though I'd known in advance that this would be a long, possibly futile process, I continued as if possessed: "I'll pop over to 20 Hillel, maybe the buildings there are older." No. 20, Hillel – I was getting closer, date-wise at least; built in 1934, permit recipient Beinish Weisler. I decided to go to lower numbers. No. 18 Hillel; built for Dr. Alec in 1934. No. 17 Hillel; permit holders Meir and Chaya Peppermeister, but the building was too new, from 1938. No. 16 Hillel; permit issued to Sugorinsky in 1941. Clearly, lower numbered houses were newer, so I went back to looking at the higher numbers. No. 24 Hillel; permit issued to Michael From in 1938. So I was playing roulette; the houses were clearly not built in any order. The next day I tried No. 14 Hillel; permit from 1950. I randomly chose No. 51 Hillel, which turned out to be the location of the city's theater. For fun I reversed the digits and looked at No. 15 Hillel – Eureka! The building permit was issued to Mayer Fellmann in September 1934. The name of the owner corresponded to what I remembered from my mother's stories, and the date was right. I was convinced that this was the address moved to from 6 Nordau. My parents resided at 15 Hillel, I didn't have any doubt. It simply felt right.

Without waiting for Sunday I immediately wrote to Hanni Amor: "... after painstaking work I discovered several facts: Since I knew from my mother's stories that my parents had lived for two years in a building that belonged to a Mayer Fellmann, I thought it might be the house on Hillel Street. I searched the original building permits of houses on Hillel St. in Haifa, to see whether there were any owned by Mayer Fellmann, and sure enough, there is one, at number 15, built in 1934. My parents apparently bought this apartment (while it was under construction) after staying for a short time (in 1934, when my mother immigrated to Palestine) in a building owned by Haim Finkelman at 6 Nordau, Haifa (a building designed by my father and built for his relatives in 1933/34). My parents must have lived at 15 Hillel until 1937, when they moved to 4 Achad

Ha'am, Haifa. I also found in the State Archives my father's file; his citizenship application, containing 11 documents, from 1937, by which time he lived at 4 Achad Ha'am. On Sunday I'll look into the books of the Hebrew Community Committee at the Tel Aviv Archives, hoping to find corroborating data there. The librarian has informed me that the material will be at my disposal as of Sunday. Next week, once I have all the information, I'll send you the official application for ownership of the property, complete with copies of the relevant documents duly certified by a lawyer."

Today I realize that it was a bit strange, to send such a letter a few days before actually visiting the Archives, but I was so proud that I did it – found the elusive address. Of course, no sooner had I clicked "Send" than I began worrying: what if I don't find my parents' address in the Tel Aviv Archives? Or if the address I find there is not 15 Hillel? Clearly, I had to find proof that does not rely on memory.

It was a tense weekend for me, trying hard not to think about my father, the lot, and addresses.

I arrived at Tel Aviv City Hall about an hour early, and treated myself to a decent cup of coffee and cake at one of the cafés in Gan Ha'Ir, the adjacent

shopping center. I was the first in line for the City
Archives. I went up to the woman in charge and
asked to see the material I'd ordered beforehand. "I
have them ready for you," she said, "old Haifa phone
books from 1935, plus two volumes of the Haifa
Hebrew Community Committee; it's the only census
done in 1935-36." The phone books looked like an
old version of the Yellow Pages. Looking through
them was fascinating, but yielded no results; I did
not find my father's name among the names of
architects who had phones in their office. So I
switched to the Electoral Register, which was luckily
arranged alphabetically. I leafed through old,
yellowing pages quickly but carefully. In Appendix I,
page 534, I found it: Shlomo Zvi Finkelman, 15 Hillel
St. And in the next line: Malia Finkelman, 15, Hillel
St. And next to those, Dr. Sima Finkelman, also at 15
Hillel St. I stared at this line, aghast. What a cruel
twist of fate! Sima, or Simka as she was called in the
family, my father's sister, the physician, was living
with them that year. Had she only been able to
adapt to life in Palestine and stayed here, she would
have been saved rather than murdered in the
Holocaust. She didn't feel safe in Palestine,
especially after the Arab attacks of August 1936 near
Haifa, where people were murdered. She left, going
back to the place where she felt safe – Chortkow –
where a few years later She met her tragic death

along with the rest of the family. This realization stunned me more than the fact that I'd found legal proof of my father's residence in 1935. There was no longer any doubt: my parents had lived at 15 Hillel St., in a house they'd bought from Mayer Fellmann. My memory had served me well once again. I asked permission to photocopy the page. The librarian looked at me curiously and said, "That's interesting... the office of the Custodian General asked for this same material a few months ago..." I smiled to myself with great satisfaction; I'd succeeded in doing the unbelievable: I found legal proof of the connection between my father and Mordechai Liebman, and my father's address in Haifa, based on original documents from seventy seven years ago.

My parents' and aunt's address
in the Electoral Register, 1935

The following day I filled out the forms sent to me by Hanni Amor and attached a statement summarizing all I knew about the past, and the information I'd accumulated in the months that had passed since attorney Elinor Kroitoru first called our home. I'd succeeded in solving the puzzle. Amazingly, once the pieces were in place, they provided a clear, unequivocal picture. Each discovery was accompanied by a document that would stand up in court, and I was certain that the picture emerging from my statement would enable me to receive the lot purchased by my father:

"I, Yaron Reshef, am the son of Shlomo Zvi Finkelman (a.k.a. Salmon Hirsh Finkelman), ID 002266294 born in Chortkow, Poland on 24 March 1908 to Yitzhak and Rivka Finkelman; and of Malia (a.k.a. Malca) Finkelman, born in Chortkow, Poland on 31 August 1911. My father died in 1958, and my mother is still alive. When he was living in Poland my father was known chiefly as Zvi or Hirsh, and once he immigrated to Palestine his name on legal documents was Shlomo Zvi Finkelman. On building plans and permits my father used to sign as Zvi Finkelman. My father graduated with a degree in architecture and building engineering in Vienna, Austria in 1929, and immigrated to Palestine on 26

December 1932 with a student visa for studying at the Technion.

During the years 1929-1932 my father worked as an architect in Poland, and was active in the Zionist movement, serving as leader in the Betar youth movement in his home town, Chortkow. My father's two closest friends in Chortkow were Mordechai Liebman and Shmuel Meiselman. Their signatures appear as witnesses on a declaration my father sent to the Technion in 1932 (see attached Appendix I – my father's declaration, signed by the witness Mordechai Liebman). Both these friends perished in the Holocaust.

After his immigration to Palestine, my father lived at several temporary addresses, while he started practicing as an architect. In July 1934 he made a trip to Poland to marry my mother, and the two returned to Palestine on October 3, 1934. Their first temporary residence was in a building owned by Haim and Heidi Finkelman at 6 Nordau St., Haifa. This building was designed and built by my father for these relatives who had immigrated from Austria. A while later, probably the end of 1934 or early 1935, my parents moved to a new apartment in Mayer Fellmann's building at 15 Hillel St., which they had bought while it was still being built. In 1937 my parents moved to 4 Achad Ha'am St., where they lived until the establishment of the State of Israel. In 1951 they moved to 20/6 Aliya St., Bat Galim, Haifa.

The apartment at 15 Hillel St. was also the home of my father's sister, Dr. Sima Finkelman, during 1935-1936. She was a GP in Poland and came to Palestine with the intention of living here, but couldn't find employment and, upset by the Arab attacks around Haifa at the time, she left the country to return to Poland in 1936. Dr. Sima Finkelman died in the Holocaust in Belzec (see attached Appendix II – my father's page of testimony at Yad Vashem about his sister's death; and Appendix III, Dr. Israel Shor's testimony at Yad Vashem about my aunt's death). I also have proof confirming my parents' and aunt's residence at 15 Hillel St., Haifa: a copy of the National Electoral Register in Haifa. The book of Haifa's Jewish residents was published by the Haifa Hebrew Community Committee in 1936. In Appendix Volume I, p. 534, the names Malca Finkelman, Dr. Sima Finkelman and Zvi Finkelman all appear as residing at 15 Hillel St. The two copies of this volume are in the National Archives and in the Tel Aviv Archives (attached as Appendix IV – photocopy of page from the book of residents with the names of my parents and my aunt.)

My father died in 1958 when I was seven. Therefore, most of my memories are from my mother's stories over the years, plus documents kept at home for many years; plus information and original documents I managed to collect recently. When I was a child, my mother used to tell us how my father bought a lot near Haifa in the early 1930s. It would seem that the lot was around current-day Tivon. She further said that it was a dream of my father and a few friends from their Zionist movement days in Chortkow, to take part in founding a Zionist settlement based on industry, which is why my father bought that lot. She used to refer to the place as Kfar Haroshet. She said that my father, who was an architect as mentioned above, designed a building which was to serve as a factory there. Years later, after my father's death, whenever we asked her where is that lot and what became of it, she'd just say that it wasn't serious and that everything changed because of the Arab attacks and because of the war. She also said that the purchase of the lot was probably related to a crooked rabbi who fled the country. It was impossible to get any more information out of her, and my sister and I treated the story as an anecdotal tale. To this day, I do not have precise information about the location of the lot. Most recently, the subject came up (for the first time in many years), when attorney Elinor Kroitoru, head of Location & Information at Hashava, The Company for Location and Restitution of Holocaust

Victims' Assets, called us in July 2011. She told us that her office had located a lot which apparently belonged to one Shlomo Zvi Finkelman of Haifa, and advised me and my sister to apply to the office of the Custodian General in the Ministry of Justice in order to continue investigating our right to that lot."

I attached all relevant documents, properly validated and certified. A week later I called the office of the Custodian General to ensure that my declaration with all accompanying documents had arrived safely. "Processing takes around six months until a final decision is made," I was told in response to my query. I didn't have any doubt as to the nature of the final decision.

***

The Family, Part I

There would now be about a five-month wait until the Office of the Custodian General made a decision about the lot. I thought that after solving the puzzle I'd be able to clear my head and no longer be so consumed by the distant past. But I remained restless. I was amazed to discover how little I knew about my family. I did not blame myself for having taken no interest in it. I was annoyed at myself for not having made an effort to get more information while it was still available. It was only natural that I accepted my mother's short, evasive replies to my questions about her family in Poland. It was a painful and loaded topic for her all those years, entwined in immeasurable guilt – the guilt of a lucky survivor where others fell victim.

A few years ago, when my mother was ninety nine years old, she confessed that she never forgave herself for living while her whole family perished in the Holocaust. Again she told me the incredible events she shared with my father. How in 1939 they left Palestine for Poland with my sister Ilana, who was then a year old, to show off their eldest daughter to their parents. They arrived at Chortkow in Galicia on the eve of World War II as German forces advanced east using blitzkrieg tactics. Their parents, especially my mother's, did all they could to convince them to stay in Poland: "War is breaking out in Europe and it'll spread. Don't leave, it is much safer here, much safer than in Palestine..." quotes my mother. After long, intense arguments, my mother almost gave in, but my stubborn father insisted. They left Chortkow on the very day of the German invasion, their train under aerial attack. When they said goodbye to their families they never imagined it would be their last goodbye. "We could have at least saved Moshe, my little brother, I will never forgive myself for not saving him," my mother said seventy-one years later, with tears in eyes.

I felt a certain obligation to myself to try and peer through the veil of time and find out what happened to my family. I knew without a doubt that most had perished in the Holocaust, but for the first time I felt that the details also mattered. Perhaps my success in solving the mystery of my father's lot convinced me that it was still possible to delve into our history and create a picture more complete than the generic "perished in the Holocaust". What happened to my family in Chortkow after my parents left in 1939? "They were forced to dig holes and were shot... that's what we found out years later from witness accounts of those who survived that hell" – my mother told me time and again. When I persisted, my mother responded somewhat automatically "There were Aktions ...what does it matter? They were rounded up and murdered..." and the topic was closed. According to my simple calculations, at least three years had passed from the time my parents left for Palestine until their families' deaths. What happened to them during that period? What were their thoughts? Their feelings? Did they know they'd been sentenced to death?

For the first time it bothered me that in a few years even the scant details I did know would fade and become part of the collective memory where nothing is personal. Holocaust memories will be unpleasant, an aesthetic blemish, but will no longer be painful. In order to feel pain one needs a personal connection to the victims. A connection that makes the historical chronicles part of your own personal narrative. I hoped that through my research I would find that connection.

In many ways the story of my family is the story of Chortkow, the town where my parents were born, where they were raised and their personalities molded. The town of Chortkow lies in a beautiful valley along the banks of the Seret River in the Ukraine. The town was surrounded by forests, the biggest and most beautiful of which was the Black Forest. The first records to mention Chortkow date back to 1427. In that year Chortkowici, the lord of the village signed his name to a letter of surrender presented to King Władysław (Vladislav) Jaeiello of Poland, in which the Polish nobility accepted the King's rule. In 1522 the lord of the manor, Jerzy Czortkowski, was given permission by King Sigismund I the Old to found the town of Chortkow. In 1578 the town was sold to Sieniawski Yiglski who built the magnificent Chortkow Castle in order to fortify and defend the town. In 1616 the town was sold to a Polish nobleman, under whom it flourished. In 1630 Count Potocki built the large wooden Church of the Ascension. In the mid-17th century (1647-1648) there were many pogroms, known as the Khmelnytsky pogroms, following which the local Jews were exiled until 1704. In 1672 the Turks conquered this part of Poland and Chortkow became the seat of the local Ottoman Pasha. The 17th century was filled with wars and battles against the Turks and Tartars. Chortkow was ruined and burned, its castle had turned to rubble and its churches to ashes. After the Treaty of Karlowitz which ended the long war between Austria and the Ottoman Empire, Chortkow was given back to the Potockis. Count Potocki allowed Jews to return to the town and in 1721 granted them rights. The Jewish community flourished and a stone synagogue was built around the remains of the old wooden one. As a result of the partition of Poland, Chortkow became part of the Austro-Hungarian Empire. In 1865 the Austro Hungarian Princess Hieronima Borkowska sold her palace in Chortkow to Rabbi David Moshe Friedman, known by the Jewish honorific as Admor, who made it his residence and the Hasidic center of Galicia. After the death of Rabbi Friedman in 1904 his son Yisroel Friedman took his place as the Hasidic leader, but moved to Vienna during World War I. Rabbi Friedman, also known as the Rabbi of Chortkow, always visited Chortkow for holidays and the city would fill with his followers who came from all over Galicia. This is the short history of Chortkow, where my parents were born. I am the son of two families, Finkelman and Kramer, which represent the two cultural poles of the Jewish community in Chortkow, and likely Galicia.

My father's family – the Finkelmans – was a well-to-do family of lumber merchants. Photos of my grandparents illustrate their typical central-European clothes and looks – an Austrian German sort of style. My grandfather Isak (Itzig) had a short beard and his payot (Jewish curly sideburns) were trimmed. The family sent their children to study in Vienna. Ethel, my father's eldest sister, mysteriously immigrated to the US and I do not have any further information about her. My Aunt Simka graduated from medical school. My Uncle Chaskel wanted to be an opera singer, but studied law instead due to parental pressure. As a student he was enamored with Zionist ideals and moved to Palestine in 1920, settled in Rosh Pina but later came down with malaria and left the country for good. My Aunt Zelda completed her PhD in philosophy and my father, Shlomo Zvi, graduated from architecture and construction studies. You can say the Finkelman family represented the Jewish Haskalah ("Enlightenment") Movement.

Rivka and Isak "Itzig" Finkelman

In comparison, my mother's family, the Kramers, were a Hasidic family. My grandfather's face, Rabbi Menachem Mendel, was covered in a heavy black beard. His face, as well as my grandmother Fradel's, wore a soft expression compared with the harsh looks of my father's parents. My mother's parents were about twenty years younger than my father's. My mother was the eldest in her family, and my father the youngest son which is why he was called Junio, meaning junior.

Menachem Mendel and Fradel Kramer

The Kramer family came from a small village named Yazlovets near Buchach, about 40 kilometers (25 miles) west of Chortkow. I suppose my mother's grandparents moved to Chortkow after they got married and had children. They likely moved to town in order to find work and improve their quality of life. As a young couple they started their own business, were successful and became wealthy. My mother described her family and life at home in her memoirs:

"I was born in 1911 in Chortkow. It is a small town in Galicia in the Ternopil province. My parents were Menachem and Fradel née Steinweiss. Their parents were also born in Chortkow. They had four children. I was the eldest. My two brothers, Anshel and Moshe, were four and five years younger than me respectively. My sister Sarah, whom we called Selka, was the youngest and 8 years my junior. [My mother did not get their ages quite right: she was the eldest, then Anshel, Selka, and Moshe was the youngest].

Aside from us, there were three young orphans who lived with us – my father's youngest siblings. Their parents died in an epidemic so my parents took them in and raised them as they raised us. It bothered me quite a bit, I was jealous of them, which happens often among children. My parents were very careful in the way they treated my father's younger siblings and whenever we quarrelled they always took their side, and I took it to heart as though my parents were against me. The orphans were Malca, Nachman and Moshe. They were a bit older than me. My parents were very well off. They were wholesalers. We had a large three-story house. Downstairs was the store which had many rooms, probably five, and the staff. There was an accountant and another five workers. They were all Jewish. My parents chose employees from families that needed the income. They gave them a job at a young age and the employees stayed at their job for many years. Even my father's brother, Baruch, who was older than the orphans who lived with us, worked and lived in that house with us. Later he got married and left. It was a wholesale store, and the customers were haberdashers (selling thread, socks, underwear etc) with their own stores in our town and other towns in the area. My parents would buy the merchandise in factories in the big cities like Lodz. They acted as agents for the factories and would sell their wares in our region.

On the second floor, right above the shop, lived our family, and the third floor was rented out to two other families. We slept two to a room, one room for my parents, one for me and my sister, and one for my two brothers. Malca had her own room. Later, when I was about ten, she was married off, with a dowry as was customary back then.   Her two brothers, the adopted orphans, shared a room as well.

Two young Christian maids also stayed in the house, as well as a Jewish cook. Father and mother both worked long hours at the store, so mother took on the Jewish cook so we could keep a kosher home. We also had a Jewish governess whose job it was to make sure that each morning we would pray and offer thanks (Modeh Ani prayer). She made sure we did our homework and didn't fight.

It was a brick house, with wood floors. The maids would polish the floor with a paste and special brushes they would wear like sandals on their feet. There were two bathtubs and several toilets. On the ground floor were a large dining room and a large kitchen. We always ate in the dining room and the servants ate in the kitchen. The kitchen had a large porcelain-tiled, wood-fired stove. We bought our bread at a kosher bakery, but always baked our challah for the Sabbath at home. On Friday they would send me to give out challah to the poor, and even when I was seeing Junio he would come along. We ate typical Jewish food at home: lokshen mit yoykh (noodle soup), with homemade noodles. We were never made to eat vegetables, and to this day I don't eat vegetables. Aspic (meat in gelatin), noodles with butter, perogies, stuffed fish, cholent (traditional Jewish stew) in the oven for the Sabbath etc. Food was prepared fresh every day. There was no fridge and food was stored in the basement. The house was located on Sobieskiego St. and on the other side of the street, not too far away, was a bus station where you could get buses to nearby towns. We had electricity in town, and the house had electric lighting.

I stayed home until I was six. There were no kindergartens. When I was six I started going to a Polish school and in the afternoons I studied in a Hebrew Jewish school where we studied Hebrew, the Old Testament and Jewish history. The classes were all in Hebrew. At home we spoke Yiddish with our parents, Polish with the maids, and amongst ourselves mostly Polish. Our morning classes were four hours, as were the afternoon classes. I knew Hebrew as well as I knew Polish. We learned Hebrew in the same accent spoken in Israel. My parents knew the holy tongue with a thick Eastern European ("Ashkenazi") accent but didn't use it regularly.

I graduated from the Polish high school, and wrote my Polish exit exams as I continued to study Hebrew. They were very strict in the Polish school. The teachers would rap our knuckles with a ruler if we were talking or otherwise disturbing the class. When we addressed the teacher we had to get up and say "Mr. Teacher". There were many punishments, like standing in the corner. The Hebrew school, in comparison, was pleasant and easy-going. Most of the students at the Polish school were Christian. Tuition was high and you had to pass a lot of exams in order to be accepted. I had Jewish friends in every class. Jews did not make friends with the Christians, who were anti-Semites. Despite that, they rarely bothered us. Classes were not co-ed, they had either boys or girls. In the Hebrew school the classes were co-ed. They weren't strict there, so we all went there willingly even though it also had exams and report cards. This was the only Hebrew school in the whole region. All the children who lived at our house went to both schools, the Polish and the Hebrew."

I knew much less about my father's family. My mother never told me anything, and I didn't ask. My only source of information was my Aunt Zelda. Zelda Finkelman, Liebling after she married Joel. She was often around at my father's home. Zelda's grandfather, Mechel, and my grandfather Itzig were brothers. When Zelda's father died in 1921 when she was only three, she and her mother and sisters moved in with my grandfather at 279 Szpitalna St. Zelda and her husband Joel were among the few who survived the Holocaust.

Zelda's sister, Zanka, was my mother's classmate and she was the one who introduced them. "... Come with me to Betar, it will be a chance to be around Junio... it's the best way to get to know him without anyone being the wiser..." my mother told me. Even after my grandfather died in 1933 Zelda stayed with them. From Zelda I learned how strict and unyielding my grandparents were: "The Finkelmans were always very stubborn, they never let anything go – not in business and not in their personal life at home..." The Finkelmans were Zionists. My Uncle Chaskel who studied law joined a group of immigrants that was known as the Student Aliya and immigrated to Palestine in 1920. After he came down with malaria he returned to Chortkow, got married and immigrated to Colombia inspired by stories of South America and Colombia from a fellow Zionist pioneer (halutz) who had travelled the world. My Aunt Simka was the girls' coordinator in Hashomer during the early '20s. She immigrated to Palestine in 1935 and returned to Chortkow about a year later. Simka continued in her Zionist activism as the on-hand doctor for many youth group activities. My father, the youngest son, was a leader in Betar and lived up to the movement's vision by immigrating to Palestine in 1932. Zelda told me that their family originally came from the town of Jagielnica. Like all Finkelmans my grandfather and his family were lumber merchants. They were well-to-do which allowed them to provide all their children with higher education. Zelda told me that my father was the mischievous one. He was always athletic and played a lot of sports. One of her favorite stories was how he came downstairs one day all the way from the top floor walking on his hands. Apparently, my grandmother had never seen anyone walking on their hands before, let alone doing so on the stairs. She tried tilting her head to correct the upside-down image, and when she saw my father holding the stairs above his head she cried that he was possessed and fainted.

I first met Zelda as a teenager, when she visited Israel. I was immediately taken with her, and whenever I traveled to the States for work I would visit her if I could. She and Joel (Lolo) would always be happy to have me and provide me some more information about our family. And so we spent hours, as she helped me write down a detailed family tree, or told me with incredible candor about what she went through during the Holocaust. How she escaped the horrors, how she hid in a bunker and lost her family. Zelda let me read the diary she wrote during the months in hiding, and was happy to answer questions. I regret all the questions I didn't ask, and have no doubt that I missed a great opportunity to find out so much more about my family and life in Chortkow as Zelda passed away in 1998 when she was only 80 years old.

One evening I sat down and summarized all the things I didn't know. This might seem odd as people usually sum up what they do know. But in this case I knew there was no one left who could provide answers and fill the gaps: Was my father's "capitalist" family forced out of their home after the Soviets occupation in 1939? They were, after all, lumber merchants and made their living from commerce. My mother never told me that her family was forced out of their beautiful house when the Soviets occupied the region. I only learned that from the address on the postcards that were sent from Chortkow to my parents in Palestine. The sender's address was now 10 Szkolna St. At first I didn't understand the reason for the change of address. Only recently, as I looked deeper into the facts, I re-read my mother's memoirs and put two and two together. The sad story became clear, starting with the expropriation of their property and eviction from their grand house to the town's outskirts. On June 6th 1941 the German army entered Chortkow. Szkolna Street was within the boundaries of the Jewish ghetto that was created after the Germans arrived, so I suppose the family was not removed from their home again. I am certain that my parents knew what their family in Chortkow was suffering in these difficult years, at least until the German occupation.

Despite my many conversations with my Aunt Zelda I never asked her when the Finkelmans were murdered. I gathered they were forced out of their home and into the ghetto with the rest of the Jews on Szpitalna Street. Thanks to my aunt, the doctor, the family probably survived until late August 1942, when everyone was sent on trains to the Belzec death camp. I found that fact in the testimony of Dr. Israel Shor who survived. He was a friend of my aunt's. I found his account regarding her fate in the testimonial pages he submitted to Yad Vashem.

My mother's parents were, in fact, a generation younger than my father's parents, which makes his parents' open-mindedness and support in providing their children with a higher education that much more remarkable. Even more so considering that they allowed their two daughters to study away from home. Sima (Simka) studied medicine, and her sister Zelda (named for her great grandmother Zelda, as was Aunt Zelda from the States) studied philosophy. Of the two girls, Sima was unusual for her time: an educated woman, with a profession, active in Zionist organizations, who remained unmarried until her death at the age of 41. Perhaps I am doing the eldest daughter, Ethel, a disservice, but as far as I know she left home at a young age and moved to the US I don't think anyone knows any more about her, other than she entered the US in 1927 and died in 1958 – information I found in US government records.

Not one of the Kramers in Chortkow survived the Holocaust. Of the Finkelmans, a few survived: Zelda Finkelman-Halstuch, my father's sister, her son Sigmund (Zigush). Zelda Finkelman-Liebling my second cousin and her husband Joel who survived together, and Eliyahu Loushu Finkelman, another second cousin. Our grandfathers were brothers. Each of them has a fascinating story to tell.

The first of our family to perish was Dr. Karl Halstuch, Aunt Zelda's husband who was a lawyer by trade. There are several accounts of his death. He was caught in the first Aktion in Chortkow, known as the Savage Aktion on August 25th, 1941. A company of the Gestapo's Flying Brigade, which just arrived in Chortkow with the Ukrainian Militia abducted a hundred Jews, some from their homes based on prepared lists, and some straight from the streets. These Jews were led to the local jail where the Germans let the doctors and pharmacists go. The rest were loaded onto trucks the next day and murdered in ditches that had been dug in advance in the Black Forest. Adam, Karl's son was caught along with his father. A speedy trial at the jail of just a few minutes ended with his release because he was too young, while his father was sentenced to death. Adam did not survive the Holocaust; he died after the family was sent to the ghetto as the result of an infection from appendicitis.

I never met my Aunt Zelda Halstuch, (Father's sister), nor her son Zigush. They were both sent to the Janowska labor camp in Lviv and were of the few in the camp who survived. After escaping the horrors, they immigrated to Colombia and lived with my Uncle Chaskel. How Zigush survived by hiding in a potato pantry, I learned from his memoirs which were posted online. He used to share his memories with students in Colombia on Holocaust remembrance days.

My Uncle Eliyahu Finkelman, Loushu, was also "lucky". While Chortkow was still under Soviet rule he was caught as a young boy, after being ratted out for hiding food or some other valuables. Loushu, the son of capitalists, was tried and sent to a jail in Siberia and so sentenced to live while his family was exterminated. It is hard to imagine what a young man, all alone, would go through in Siberia. But fate is a fickle mistress and he got to keep his life.

As for Aunt Zelda Finkelman-Liebling's story, I knew it well. Her family was sent to a labor camp from which people would be sent to death camps for extermination. Her husband Joel, a dentist by trade, treated the camp staff. Before the camp was liquidated and all its inmates killed the camp commander allowed Joel to choose who would be allowed to escape with him – his wife Zelda or his sister. Joel chose Zelda. Zelda and Joel escaped, leaving their family behind. Zelda's diary, written in their bunker-hideaway after their escape provides a glimpse into a terrible world full of inconceivable physical and mental hardships. Half of her diary was lost during the war, but the other half survived along with Zelda. Zelda and Joel immigrated to the US and had two children: Mordechai and Linette.

Digging into our family history took up a lot of my free time. I felt the need to create a memorial for my parents' families. I had a collection of family photos of those who were no longer with us. When I found a website dedicated to the memory of the Jewish community in Chortkow, founded by Miri Gershoni the daughter of Chortkow survivors, I decided it was the right place to pay tribute to my family's memory. I began scanning the photos, making sure I knew who was who and relevant dates so I could add descriptions to the photos. Once again I opened the family tree I made that night with Aunt Zelda in New Jersey. Suddenly each name had a face, I knew how different people were connected to one another, which ones were friends, and each photo told its own story.

In July 2012, my sister Ilana forwarded to me a letter from Miri Gershoni with questions about our family. The timing was perfect; I had just that day finished scanning the photos and adding a few words to each one. I contacted Miri and a few days later we met at my home. It was a fascinating meeting. I was impressed and moved by the task Miri took upon herself to document and commemorate the community of Chortkow. I was happy to share everything I knew of my family, and happier still to make this connection which allowed me to find out more about them. After a couple of days I organized all my material and sent it to Miri. I was amazed by her dedication and hard work, as she uploaded the photos and descriptions the very next day.

Even more incredible were the events of the next few days. While Raya and I were on a trip to Acadia National Park in Maine, I received an email from Miri:

"Is Pepe Kramer part of your family? I have a number of photos in Tonka (Tonia's) Sternberg's collection (on the website) with the name Pepe Kramer written on them. I'm sending them to you. Tonka Sternberg also has a picture of Moshe Kramer that is an exact copy of the one you have. I assume then that Pepe is a relative of your mother's."

I was stunned by the email. I had no idea who Pepe Kramer was. I got online immediately and found the memorial page for the families Sternberg and Vermuth on the Chortkow website. Next to photo #10 it said: "... Moshe Kramer, a good friend of Tonia. His sister, Pepe Kramer was her best friend. Both came from a large wealthy family of which no one survived." This was incredible – finding a picture of my Uncle Moshe on the page of another family. I had no idea who Pepe Kramer was. I assumed it was a nickname of my Aunt Selka's or that I'd found another of my mother's sisters whom I'd never heard of, but that seemed unlikely.

So we went walking in Acadia, Raya and I; my eyes seeing the beautiful landscape, but my mind busy with this puzzle. It wasn't Selka... Selka was two years older than Moshe and I don't think they were both friends with the same girl. In addition, Pepe seemed like a nickname for another person, it didn't "feel" like it belonged to Selka. I thought that had it been Selka's nickname it would have come up somehow, I would have heard it from my mother, or it would have appeared in her memoirs.

When we came back from our hike I quickly checked the memorial website and the photos again. I wrote to Miri:

"... This is very strange... Moshe Kramer is certainly my uncle. It is the exact same photo that I sent you. His sister is Selka Kramer though, not Pepe. Possibly her nickname was Pepe, but I've never heard it before. Moshe Kramer had no other sisters except my mother and their sister Selka. There was one more cousin at home that they had adopted, but she was older than my mother. The strange thing is the wording on that web page: "Moshe Kramer, a good friend of Tonia... Both came from a large wealthy family of which no one survived." How could they not know that my mother (Moshe's sister) was living in Haifa all these years? How could Tonia, who published these photos, not know that?"

The following morning Miri's reply was waiting in my inbox:

Tonia Vermuth née Sternberg lives in a senior living complex in Haifa: Dor Carmel. She is in full possession of her faculties and you can simply talk to her. She has two daughters about our age... I will get you her phone number. I can't find it right now, but you can reach her daughter, Hanna Avni, by email..."

I wrote to Hanna that day and asked if it would be possible to ask her mother some questions about my mother's family, about Moshe, Selka, and whether she was Pepe. I also asked if Tonka knew what happened to my mother's family. The next day Hanna responded:

"Hi Yaron, I just got off the phone with my mother. She remembers the family. Moshe Kramer was her classmate. I will find out more when I visit her and will let you know. Best, Hanna."

On Saturday evening I received another email: "Hi Yaron, last night I visited my mother armed with all the material your family published online. I arrived with mixed feelings, knowing it is emotionally taxing for her to talk about the past. My mother is the only survivor of a large, established family, who bravely and heroically survived many hardships on top of the traumas during the first years of the war when she was still with her family. Talking about these topics has always made her sad and brings up emotions that deprive her of sleep for days, so as her family we try to do so as little as possible. My mother knew your parents, especially your mother, and what little she told me about them corresponds with what you wrote. She also said she spent a lot of time at the Kramers' as she was friends with Pepe and Moshe, who were her age. Her parents also knew your grandparents on your mother's side. She says they were extraordinary people in their lives, in the values they lived by and the respect they afforded every man, including of course adopted family members, and the adopted daughter Pepe. It seems I was wrong when I wrote that Selka's nickname was Pepe, so the picture's description should be amended. The person in the photo is Pepe, a close friend of my mother's. I quote: "Moshe would come over to our house and to the store every day. Pepe, the adopted daughter they treated just like their own, was my good friend and Moshe was also part of this friendship. On holidays they wanted her to go home and see her poor mother and orphan brothers, but she didn't want to and only did so because she had no choice." My mother also says one of the two families that lived upstairs in the rented flat was the Greenberg family. Weddings were held in a place called Bristol and your parents probably got married there. My mother remembers well when your mother came to visit with the baby. My mother visited her often. She was 16 at the time, and remembers also when they went back to Palestine. My mother also remembers Zelda, but not Simka the doctor. The most interesting part of the story she told at the very end of our conversation: The family hid in a bunker (shelter?) with a door that had to be closed from the outside and then locked from the inside. Pepe sacrificed herself for them; she went out to close the door and was then discovered and killed. That's how those who were inside were also discovered. Moshe was the one to come and close the door to our bunker. The families were close and each felt the need to help the other... in the end they were all killed. The Nazis flooded the bunker and drowned them. My mother wasn't in the bunker, and maybe that's why she survived. Best to you and your family, Hanna."

Wow. I did not expect such a letter. A short and concise description of the murder of my mother's family came from an unexpected source and with very little effort on my part. Again I felt that no sooner do I think of a missing piece of information than I promptly receive the answer in a surprising and unforeseen manner. I had no doubt that this was indeed how my mother's family came to their end, though a year ago I had different reports that told of the murder of my grandfather Menachem Mendel Kramer. At that time my sister bought me Marta Goren's book Voices from the Black Forest, a detailed and chilling account of the extermination of Chortkow's Jews. In the book I found an account of the murder of a man named Mendel Kramer:

"On the night between the 26th and 27th of August 1942 the first evacuation Aktion took place in Chortkow. In this Aktion Jews were sent by train to the Belzec death camp. About 2,500 Jews were sent to their death. After the Aktion the bodies of 500-600 murdered Jews were strewn in the ghetto and town streets. When the Aktion was over, a few Jews were selected to gather the corpses. Three teams were formed, each with two Gestapo soldiers and one Jew... Mendel Kramer, a 65 year-old Jew, was among those to collect the bodies and pile them in the market square. Albert Brettschneider, of the Gestapo, ordered him to turn around and without reason shot him in the head."

As far as I know my grandfather was the only Mendel Kramer in Chortkow, but I could be wrong. So at first, I accepted this account of my grandfather's murder. That Gestapo officer was tried in Mannheim in 1974 and was sentenced to 20 years in jail, and likely died behind bars. After a more thorough examination though, the age of the man in the story did not fit my grandfather. My grandfather was born in 1890, so on the day of the Aktion he would have been only 52, not 65. I suppose the man who gave his account of the event knew Mendel Kramer or he wouldn't have mentioned his age, but I could be wrong. That's why Tonia's account "felt right", true and more reliable. Her close acquaintance with my family left no doubt in my heart regarding my mother's family's tragic end.

A cynic might say that I could choose for myself one tragic end or the other, and I chose to believe the reliable information I received in that most unexpected way.

I completed the puzzle using the new information I gathered and other bits and pieces to fill in the blanks; first with regards to Pepe, the new character who was now part of my family. Pepe was supposedly twelve years younger than my mother. Seeing as my mother first left Chortkow in 1934, and seeing as Pepe would have been about eleven at the time, it is likely that my mother didn't know her well and did not think of her as an integral part of the family. Maybe that's the reason she never mentioned Pepe in her family stories. To the best of my knowledge, Mother's parents' home gradually emptied during the '30s and her parents, following family tradition, decided to adopt "a new daughter". I suppose that Pepe had lost her father, or that her poor family could not afford her school tuition, which would have been exceedingly expensive at the time so it is possible that my mother's parents decided to act as they had done before, and provide the girl with a new life, an education and financial stability. I believe Pepe came from Yazlovets near Buchach, where my grandfather's family was originally from. I am certain that the mere fact that Tonia remembered my parents' visit in Chortkow in 1939 shows that the two girls, 16 year-old Pepe and Tonia, enjoyed playing with my sister Ilana, the baby who came to Chortkow from Palestine and must have been a bit of an "attraction". Tonia also remembers parting with my parents, after which the world turned upside down. The memorial webpage for Tonia Sternberg's family was like a window allowing me a peek into the past. The photos told a story of a different life, friendship among girls rowing a boat down the Seret River, or proudly posing for the camera in sweaters they had just finished knitting.

Tonia Sternberg (right) and Pepe Kramer (left)
on the Seret River

Once I was able to absorb the new information and form a narrative that I thought made sense, I quickly responded to Hanna's email:

"I am replying this late only because of the time difference, I am currently in the US. Many thanks for your letter, I was deeply touched. Please send my thanks to your mother as well. I am sure that bringing up these difficult memories is not easy for her or for yourself. I admire the people who were able to survive that hell, and build a new life and new families. It makes any difficulties we experience in our lives seem trivial by comparison. The information your mother provided sheds some light on the "black hole" that is my family history. My mother is about 12 years older than your mother. When my mother first left Chortkow for Palestine in 1934, her younger brother Moshe was about 12, approximately the same age as your mother and Pepe. From the stories I've heard over the years there were probably more orphans in the Kramer household, just as there were at the Finkelman household, my father's family. Most likely Pepe Kramer arrived at the house after my mother left for Palestine in 1934. Chances are she came from a place called Yazlovets (Jazłowiec in Polish). Yazlovets was close to Buchach and about 50km from Chortkow. I know that's where the Kramers were from originally and that they had relatives in Yazlovets. If your mother remembers the name of the town Pepe came from or where she went on holidays (against her wishes) that mystery would be solved. I know for a fact that, during the Soviet occupation, the Kramers moved from, or were forced out of, their large house on Sobieskiego St. to a house at 10 Szkolna St. They may have moved a few more times in the following years. I was able to deduce that much from the return-address on the postcards they sent my mother after the Soviet occupation. The Greenberg family you mentioned in your email, may have lived in the Kramer's first house or one of the others. As for how my mother's family met their end, this is completely new information to me. I was vaguely aware of hidden bunkers and tunnels, from stories that Zelda Finkelman-Liebling told me, but I had never heard such a stark description of the end of the Kramer family. It is both horrifying and moving. It is incredible to think that your mother, Pepe and Moshe had a normal life as teenagers and I am every bit as curious about their everyday normal life as I am about the war, its horrors and devastation. I wish I had that information. My mother and her family lost touch in 1940 when the letters and postcards stopped. So we have nothing about the family after the war broke out in 1939 and my parents left with my sister for Palestine. In fact, we have no information about the day-to-day life of the Kramer family from 1934 to 1939. Mother told us nothing. It's possible that she herself didn't know. My mother, who loved her little brother Moshe dearly, never forgave herself for not taking him along when they fled back to Palestine. These thoughts haunted her till the last days when I was still able to communicate with her. This month she'll turn 101, but I'm afraid she no longer responds, so I can't converse with her. All her life Mother felt guilty for surviving while her whole family died. Hanna, I thank you for this important, fascinating and touching information. Best of health to your mother, and comfort from her family. I think I sound like someone who had a proper Chortkowic upbringing. I would be delighted with any additional scrap of information. And of course a special thanks to Miri – she deserves all the credit for this riddle. Yaron"

The next morning I got another reply from Hanna. This time her email contained files of memoirs written by her mother, Tonia. The content was horrific, it shed light on that dark period of persecution and extermination of the Jews of Chortkow as experienced by a nineteen-year-old girl. Tonia's accounts and memories were a stark contrast to the pastoral peace of the photos. A contrast that only heightened the tragedy.

Within Tonia's memoirs, I found the horrifying description of her brother's murder. I might not have included this account, but I found two contradicting details referring to the same events. In one account, Tonia's sister appears to be the one who helps to bury her brother's body, but at other points she tells her family that her close friend, probably Pepe, is the one who helped. I chose to include this account, without any additional attempt to confirm who helped Tonia, for it's clear to me that even if Pepe was not there in person, she was there in spirit, her closest friend, sharing everything Tonia went through. They were good friends and shared this terrible tragedy. Tonia wrote:

"A few weeks before Passover, in March 1942, the Seret River overflowed from the snowmelt and flooded Mr. Weiser's new flour mill. The grain in the storerooms on the ground floor got wet. Jews were ordered to remove the wet sacks of grain and carry them to the upper levels. My brother volunteered for this task. The German SS men supervised the Jewish workers, abused them and made them run as they carried the sacks. Those who struggled were beaten half to death. My brother was a strong, healthy man and he excelled at this chore. He and his friends would help other Jews. Mr. Drohowicer told us that my brother carried his sacks as well. Two SS men, who saw my brother at work, were impressed by his abilities and his willingness to help so invited him to row the boat they used to cross the surging river. When, in the middle of the river, one of them bent over and rocked the boat. The SS men then accused my brother of trying to drown them and one of them shot and killed him. When everyone came back from work, and my brother still had not returned, my mother had a feeling that something bad happened. She was so wracked with worry that she had a heart attack. She kept mumbling "my son is gone, my son is gone..." That night we learned my brother was one of three victims who were murdered that day. Early the next morning Frimka (my sister) and I went and pulled my brother's body out of the water with great difficulty. Not only was he a large strong man, but his body was waterlogged. We carried him together, off the beaten track, and buried him in the cemetery.

His death was a harsh blow. He was a gentle man, always willing to help his fellow man and, around there, were many people who needed help. That was the reason he had volunteered, in the early days, to the Judenrat Police..."

It was Friday, December 28 2012. As I was driving, back from an early get together with friends, I heard the horoscopes on the radio. It said Virgos are experiencing an improvement in their health, and they are at their best. I smiled to myself and decided to change my morning plans. I went to visit my mother. As I was driving, I thought it was time for her to say a few words, after a silence of a year and a half. When I arrived at the nursing home I found my mother looking at me, her eyes open. When I said "Hi, Mom," she responded clearly "I'm happy to see you." I led her in a wheelchair to a quiet corner and tried to get her to talk. When I got home I wrote to Hanna and Miri:

"I visited my mother today at the nursing home. She's been unresponsive for a year and a half. Most of this time she just sat there with her eyes closed, and hasn't spoken a word. She is a hundred and one years old and three months. I told her how you told me about your mother Tonia, and that for the first time I'd heard of Pepe Kramer. I asked her, "Who was Pepe Kramer?" She opened her eyes and lucidly answered, "Pepe was Tonia's best friend. She lived with my father and mother after we left... she was a little girl." We talked in the dining hall where the morning activities take place. The nursing staff present were all surprised. I loaded a picture of Pepe, your mother and another friend from the Chortkow website on my iPhone and asked my mother to try and recognize the people in the photo (her eyesight is fine). When I pointed to Pepe my mother said her name, and when I pointed to your mother she very clearly said "that's Tonia." She did not recognize the third girl in the photo. I then showed her the photo of Pepe and Tonia in the boat and asked her where it was taken. Without a moment's hesitation she replied "the Seret River." Long story short, it was an amazing, totally unexpected experience. I thought you might like to know..."

On August 6th, 2012 I received an email and photo from Miri.

"I'm enclosing a group photo of my father's friends who went out to the woods together to have this picture taken before he left for Eretz Israel in the fall of 1936. Among the people in the photo is your uncle, Moshe Kramer. My father is in the back row, third from the left. Moshe is wearing the Polish high school uniform. Jewish students in Chortkow were slowly being pushed out of the Polish school because of the numerus clausus law (a limit on the percentage of Jewish students in Universities). This means he was an excellent student and the family had the money to pay the outrageous tuition Jews were charged. For that reason the Jewish school was founded a year later in 1937. In 1938 it was recognized by the authorities as a Jewish public school with its own public school uniform and badge. I think classes stopped with the Russian occupation, but I'm not sure. My father didn't study at the Polish school, which is why he did not wear the typical uniform. My father told me, as it also says in your mother's memoirs, that the Kramer family lived across from the bus station. I currently don't have any photos of it, but when I come across one I will send it along. My mother translated some of your postcards, the parts written in Polish. If you go into Letters at The Kramer Family on the website you will find her translation..."

Moshe Kramer, front row third from the right. 1936

I could easily identify my uncle. A smiling, good looking boy who looked exactly as he did in my mother's photos. The hard part was reading the partial translations of the postcards my parents received after returning to Palestine. Chortkow had already been under Soviet rule for a year when the postcards were sent. The return address had changed after the family business was expropriated and they were cast out of their home and had to move to Szkolna St. The letters are in Yiddish and Polish. Mendel Kramer wrote in Yiddish, and Selka, my mother's sister, wrote in Polish. Here is the translation of the Polish:

January 1940: My dears, since our dear father left me no space I simply send kisses. Sela

March 1940: "Dearest ones, last week we received your postcard and we were delighted. Thank you. We are grateful that you are well. We are the same. Our lives continue and that is all. Why do you not write? Tell us whether Junio has work and what kind of work it is? Is he making any money? How is our dear Ilana? Does she miss us as we miss her? Write to us at length and tell us all about it. Wishing you a happy holiday and sending kisses. Sela. Have a kosher Passover."

The last postcard from July 10th 1940: "I thank you for the photos, thank the lord... we are lucky... you are lucky that you made it to Palestine. We are all healthy. Junio, I ask that you write to us about everything, how Ilana is growing, and what she says. She is our great joy and comfort. Kisses. S Kramer. Chortkow."

This partial translation was enough to make the family's feelings abundantly clear. The despair they felt, trapped under a hostile Soviet regime that saw them as enemies of the revolution. These were the last words from Chortkow. Then there was only silence. Infinite silence.

My parent's visit to Chortkow with Ilana 1939, from right to left: Ilana, Rivka Finkelman, Dr. Sima Finkelman, Mom, Selka Kramer

***

The Lot, Part II

On April 25, 2012 I received a letter from the office of the Custodian General:

Re: Property registered to Shlomo Zvi Finkelman

The authorized committee in our office discussed the release application submitted by you and decided to grant your request and release said property.

The property, half of parcel 40 in block 11398, was transferred to the State's hands in 1996 – attached is a copy of the order.

In order to release the property, you must apply to the Israel Land Administration, Acquisition & Expropriation Department, 15 HaPalyam Blvd, ground floor, P.O.Box 548, Haifa 33095.

For your information, the number of the parcel was changed several times, and at present it is part of parcel 197 in block 11398 (it was combined with another parcel, and its area is 3,121 square meters).

Sincerely,

Shira Gordon, Atty.,
Attorney for the Custodian General

I felt great. I succeeded in doing the impossible. I completed the circle; an action begun by my father and Mordechai Liebman in 1935 has been completed by me. Part of the lot purchased by my father is being returned to its legal owners. My euphoria was somewhat dampened by the fact that Mordechai Liebman apparently had no beneficiaries. I still hope that when this story is published, it may lead to finding any remaining relatives of Mordechai's.

The first thing I immediately did was try to locate the lot. With the help of my partner, Hanan, and the Land Administration website, we located the lot within minutes. The original lot had been combined with other lots in this block and re-divided, but the actual location had not changed: in Kiryat Haroshet ("industrial town"), an area of Tivon on the southern slopes of the hills facing Mt. Carmel along the Kishon River. Just coming across the name Kiryat Haroshet set the bells ringing – it was so similar to the name I recalled from my mother's stories and my childhood memories. I'd remembered it as Kfar Haroshet ("industrial village"), as I wrote in the declaration submitted to the Custodian General, but it turned out the accurate name is Kiryat Haroshet. Also, from my mother's stories, I remembered the character of a crook; as it turned out, there was a rabbi involved in the history of settlements in that region, but judging from the information I now found, he was a tragic figure, far from a crook.

Location of the lot in Kiryat Haroshet
(marked by a pin)

Rabbi Yehezkel Taub of Yablona began selling the Kiryat Haroshet lands in 1933 for 37 lira per dunam (1000 m²). On Lag Ba'Omer (a Jewish holiday occurring around mid-May) of 1934 the cornerstone to Kiryat Haroshet was laid, named after the biblical "Harosheth Hagoyim", the dwelling place of Sisera, captain of the army of Jabin king of Canaan (Judges 4:2). Opinions regarding the location of the biblical Harosheth Hagoyim are divided; some think it was at present-day Amakim Junction or near Yokneam. Other scholars think Harosheth Hagoyim was an early name of the forested mountains in the north of the country rather than the name of a single city involved in industry or craft. According to these scholars, Harosheth Hagoyim is the woodland that used to stretch from Jezreel Valley northward to the Galilee.

The young rabbi, living with his followers in Yablona, Poland, wanted to become a Zionist entrepreneur and bring his followers along to Palestine, to take part in redeeming the land. In 1924 Rabbi Taub established in Warsaw a company to sell land, called Nachlat Yaacov. Through the mediation of Zionist leader Yehoshua Hankin, Taub bought some land on the Sheikh Abreik hills from Hachsharat Hayishuv (The Jewish Palestine Land Development Company). The original land owner was a Lebanese Christian named Sursock. After the purchase, Rabbi Taub began selling plots of land to his followers, and established a Hassidic agricultural settlement called Nachlat Yaacov. But the settlement could not cope with the day-to-day hardships. Security and financial difficulties proved to be too much for the Hassidic settlers, so they turned to the JNF (Jewish National Fund) and asked them to exchange the treacherous land for other lots more suitable for settling. The swap took place: Rabbi Taub returned to the JNF all the land he'd bought to sell, and in return received new land on which his followers established an agricultural village called Kfar Hassidim. This stretch of land was both more fertile and further away from hostile Arab villages, which enabled the new settlement to flourish.

However, despite his obligation to JNF, Rabbi Taub did not return all the Sheikh Abreik lands to JNF, but kept for himself a lot of some 900 dunam (~222 acres) on the slopes of the hills opposite Mt. Carmel, along the Kishon River. The rabbi, who had a shrewd business sense as any modern day real estate developer, felt that despite the inhospitable topography and marshes in the land he held, it was worth his while hanging on to it and trying to sell lots for the construction of a new, urban-rural settlement. He believed that the railway, the western route of the Jezreel Valley railway, would enable people to live in a rural environment yet work in the city of Haifa, which was only a half-hour's train ride away. In his vision, he saw a place where people would grow and consume their own fruit and vegetables, strengthening the rural aspect of their lives, while being employed or owning a business in Haifa. The rabbi also tried to attract light industry to the area, such as metal workers, textile and upholstery workers, and so develop a town based on the model of rural towns in central Europe.

Rabbi Taub succeeded in selling dozens of lots for building, but still the settlement did not flourish. The new immigrants, scared of the nearby Arab and Beduin population, preferred living in the big cities. The tension reached its peak after the murder of two Jewish guards who were guarding a pool nearby, close to today's Yokneam, and the development of the settlement came to a halt. But Taub did not give up. He imported two shiploads of lumber, had some forty portables built, and embarked on a new marketing campaign: Buy a dunam of land and receive another dunam, a wooden cabin, a grant of two lira a month, and free transportation to Haifa. This campaign was a success, the settlement developed, and by the end of 1937 comprised of 460 families. In addition, there were two small factories; one for hats and one for shaving brushes, kindergartens, where a school and synagogue were built. Reality came even closer to Taub's vision when the railways opened a special commuter line, with two trains; morning and afternoon, providing residents working in Haifa with convenient transportation to work and back, all for a monthly ticket costing 40 grush (0.40 lira). It seemed like a huge success story, until all hopes were dashed tragically. On the night of June 20th, 1938, a gang of Arabs raided the settlement shooting everywhere indiscriminately, burning down the school and the synagogue, and torching houses with their residents inside. Three of the Gutterman family and two of the Spiegel family were burned alive. The residents immediately started fleeing. The Valley train stopped at the settlement every half hour, picking up the fleeing residents and their baggage. Forty-eight hours later there were only a dozen people left in the settlement out of eight hundred. Kiryat Haroshet did not recover for sixty years.

Rabbi Taub got in over his head financially. The clerks working under him may have stolen what was left of his money. He couldn't make his loan payments, and in 1938 the Magistrates Court in Haifa ordered that his assets be sold to cover part of his debts. Taub escaped to the US, abandoned religion, changed his name to George Nickel and worked as a real estate developer and contractor in Los Angeles. In 1980 Taub returned to Israel, went into a retirement home in Afula, and re-adopted religion. In May 1986, at age 91, he died and was buried in the section of the early Hassidim in the cemetery of Kfar Hassidim, the village which he had established.

The correlation between my childhood memories, the discovery of Father's and Mordechai's ownership of the lot, and the info I gathered about Kiryat Haroshet were fascinating and shed light on my father's actions in buying the lot. I have no doubt that Rabbi Yehezkel Taub's initiative to build a rural-industrial community connected to Haifa by rail was the talk of the town among town planners, architects and pioneering settlers in the Haifa region of 1934. Though there was a construction boom in and around Haifa in those days, this project was definitely unique.

The official notice states the place and date of the auction, the sum of the debt 24.646 Israeli Lira [Palestine pounds], and the terms of sale. The items listed: a Hebrew Remington typewriter; a calculating machine, two office desks, and five chairs.

Rabbi Taub, originally from Poland, marketed the lands especially to the Jewish middle class of Haifa and Poland. The idea of combining rural living with commercial enterprise and setting up industrial plants was very attractive to people who saw this model as one enabling them a lifestyle similar to what they had in their homeland. Father, who left Palestine for Poland that year in order to propose to

my mother, must have told his close friends and
Betar activists in Chortkow about Taub's enterprise.

הודעה בדבר מכירת מטלטלין

ליהוי ידוע שנתנה החלטה ע"י נשיא
ההוצאה לפועל של ביהמ"ש זה בדבר
מכירת פומבית של החפצים המעוקלים
ברשומה הבאה. לכסוי ההוג לפי פסק־
דין מבית משפט השלום בחיפה במשפט
מס' 4595/37 אורחי על סך 24.646
לא"י בצירוף הוצאות וכו'. בטקרת שלא
נתן פקודת דחיה, המכירה תתקיים
ע"י חא' אברהם יעקב אלקאים ביום
ד' שחל ביום 26 לאיקטובר 1938. חמ־
כירה. התחיל ב־3 אחה"צ.

ואלה הם תנאי המכירה: א) החפצים
הנמכרים ימסרו לקונה אחרי תשלום
הסכום המוצע חמזו על ידו ; ב) אם הקונה
יסרב לקחת את החפצים שנמכרו לו
יימכרו. שנית ופקיד ההוצאה לפועל יובה
מאת הקונה את ההפרש במחיר אם
הסכום המוצע במכירה חשניה יהיה
פחות ; ג) אם יהיה צורך אפשר יהיה
לדרוש מהמציעים במכירה הפומבית
בשחון של עשרה אחוז מסכום הצעתם,
ד) שכר המכריז חל על הקונה וישולם
בזמן מכירת החפצים למציע את המחיר
הכי גבוה ובזמן מסירתם לו, ה) על
הקונה להוציא את החפצים שנקנו על
ידו על חשבונו מהמקום שנמכרו בו
תו"מ אחרי שימסרו לו ע"י המכריז,
אם לא יוצאו החפצים ישארו במקום
המכירה על אחריות הקונה, ו) אפשר
לקבל פרטים נוספים מאת מר אברהם
יעקב אלקאים במשרד ההוצאה לפועל
בחיפה, הפקיד הסמונה על מכירח זו.

רשימת החפצים המוצאים למכירה:
מכנת כתיבה רסין־מון עברית, מכונת
מספרים, שני שלחנות משרד, 5 כס־
אות, יימכרו במרכז מכחרי חשן, ברה'
חמרובי בחיפה.
                      4.10.38

נשיא שופט השלום

A notice in the daily Davar: the bailiff's notice
regarding the auctioning of Taub's effects to cover
his debts.

Father and his good pal Mordechai Liebman then decided on jointly buying a lot for the purpose of building an industrial plant of some sort. Father returned to Israel with Mother, and bought the lot jointly with Mordechai.

As pleased with myself as I was for completing the puzzle, I was rather shaken by certain thoughts that pervaded my consciousness. Thoughts about the residents of Kiryat Haroshet, many of whom had recently arrived from Poland, weighed on my mind. They'd come to start a new life, only to go through the trauma of attacks complete with the burning of schools, synagogues and houses with their inhabitants. But, this time, the attackers were not Poles, Cossacks or Ukrainians, but local Arabs and Beduin. I have no doubt that in the subconscious of many of these residents there lurked a post-traumatic experience of persecution and attacks, which they were now re-living. That may have been the reason that most of the settlement's residents never returned, and the place was deserted for decades.

I never found the plans for the structure Father had designed for that lot, and it is obvious it was never built. I can't be sure why, but I can well imagine. My father probably put all his energy into designing apartment buildings in Hadar Hacarmel neighborhood and never got around to that project. Or maybe Taub's failure to sell the other lots during 1935-36 cooled Father's enthusiasm. Later, once the place was deserted due to the attacks, the lot lost its value, became irrelevant and was forgotten over time. The copy of the official papers I received from the Land Registry after the Custodian General confirmed my ownership of the lot and provided the exact location, showed that only in 1954 was the lot registered to my father and Mordechai Liebman in equal parts. What I couldn't understand was why the Custodian General registered half the lot to my father and the other half to the name of a person who died in the Holocaust. I never considered the possibility that my father wasn't aware that the lot was officially put in his name well after the actual purchase -- in fact, only about four years before his death.

On the other hand, the new-found knowledge of the lot's precise location shed new light on old evidence that had been right in front of my nose. In my mother's collection of photos, there was one taken in 1945, where my parents and sister are sitting on a rock in mountainous terrain very similar to that of Kiryat Haroshet. On the back of the photo it says, "The lot that never was."

Following the instructions of the Custodian General, I contacted the offices of the Israel Land Administration (ILA) in Haifa. The manager I reached politely put me through to her deputy who would guide me through the bureaucratic tangle. Friends had warned me of the difficulty in dealing with the ILA, but I found their attitude to be extremely fair, courteous and helpful. Yafit Elad, deputy manager in charge of acquisition, exchange and expropriation for Haifa & its environs, kindly explained to me all the steps needed to be taken and the documents I needed to submit, for them to hand over the property to me, or, alternatively, buy it from me. The process which began in early May 2012, ended nine months later. During that time, not once did I have to actually go to their offices: all communication was conducted by phone and email, with the utmost efficiency and empathy. I am sure that my endeavors to return to my family a lot lost seventy seven years earlier aroused empathy. I was given all the guidance and assistance necessary, not once being asked to hire the services of an appraiser or a lawyer.

On the afternoon of February 17th, 2013 a sum equal to the appraised value of the lot was deposited in my bank account, as per the agreement between the ILA and the beneficiaries of Shlomo Zvi Finkelman, whom I represented.

Even though the story of the lost lot had seemingly ended, and I received its full value to my satisfaction, I was curious to know how come it had disappeared for so many years and why it got the nickname "the lot that never was". So one morning, equipped with all the documents plus Attorney Shira Gordon's letter confirming my ownership of the lot, I went over to the Land Registry offices at Haifa's Ministry of Justice. I'd spoken to them earlier on the phone in an attempt to locate the lot's original bill of sale. Following that conversation, I managed to print out the lot's historical land registry records via the internet. The land registration record showed that my father's and Mordechai's ownership of the land was registered only in 1954, nineteen years after they bought it. I was surprised to learn that this ownership was revoked by the court and reverted to the Custodian General in March 1997.

I completed the application form to receive a copy of the property file according to the lot number I had and the helpful clerk checked my application on the computer. Within minutes she said to me in wonder: "This is a strange entry. There is no ID number next to the person whom you claim is your father, and no ID number next to the other owner... I can't give you any information regarding this entry because I can't verify your connection to the historical owner of this property... Moreover, the land reverted from them back to the Custodian General in 1997." I replied that I was aware of all that, but as things stand, the Custodian General returned the ownership of the land to my family, and any day now we were supposed to get a sum equal to the value of the lot from the Israel Land Administration, according to a written agreement. I showed the clerk the relevant documents, but to no avail. I asked to see the Registrar herself to explain and show her the documents. It took some assertiveness on my part to get in, but she was firm: "I cannot identify the owners nor your connection to them without ID numbers next to their names... Ask whoever handled your case at the Custodian General to write to me with all the details, and we'll see what can be done..."

I left with an uncomfortable feeling. For a whole year I investigated, sought and produced evidence that my father owned this lot, but the wheels of bureaucracy seem to have turned back, sending me to square one, where I'm requested to prove who my father is, and that he's the same Shlomo Zvi Finkelman who is registered as the land owner. The registrar apologized and said she must be extra careful because there are many cases of identity theft and fraud in matters to do with land ownership registration. Some two hours later the fax at home rang, and the machine produced a confirmation that the ILA had transferred the funds to my bank account.

I was curious, and wanted to see the original bill of sale or sales contract which should have been attached to the property abstract – the full information about the land owner/s, as it appears in the Land Registry – in order to study the history of the lot: Was it really bought directly from rabbi Yehezkel Taub or Nachlat Yaacov, the company he owned? On what date? And why was the lot "lost" over so many years? Clearly there had been some bureaucratic mix-up, since my parents never paid any taxes on the lot, which to me meant one thing only: the lot was no longer theirs.

The next day I wrote a short letter reporting on my visit to the Haifa Land Registry Office and sent it to Attorney Shira Gordon at the Custodian General's. I took that opportunity to thank her for all her efforts to return the lot to my family and having us reimbursed for it. Impatient as I was, I called Shira, who said that it is contrary to current procedures to give copies of the bill of sale or sales contract to interested parties; but in her opinion this was an unusual case. Since the lot was legally transferred to my ownership, and I agreed to give it back to the ILA in return for proper remuneration which was already carried out, there was no risk of my misusing the documents in question. She'd have the file brought up from Archives, request approval, and do her best. I was certain my request would be granted. So far the Custodian General's office was fair and empathic in handling my case, so I couldn't see any reason for them not to. I had to wait two long days before receiving the unforeseen reply.

Dear Mr. Yaron Reshef,

I received the file this morning and went through it. It appears that we have no bill of sale or any Land Registry document bearing your father's signature.

Your father bought the land through Nachlat Yaacov Co. Once the company went into dissolution and receivership, all its creditors were investigated, as well as anyone who had bought real estate through it but had not yet been registered as its owner; and in this context your father's name came up. In other words, the information about your father's ownership came from the receivers of Nachlat Yaacov Co., and that company's records. Once we were officially in charge, we took steps to register ownership in his name. I've scanned the receivership document containing information about your father and his partner, for your perusal.

Regards,

Shira Gordon, Attorney at Law.

The first thought that came to mind was: Eventually justice was done; after 78 years Father got full ownership of the land he'd bought. Suddenly everything fell into place; Shira's document shed new light on the issue. It completely supported my mother's story of the "crooked rabbi", or – as I now see him – a Zionist real estate entrepreneur, who got into financial trouble because of the Jewish-Arab conflict in Palestine. The dissolution of Nachlat Yaacov Ltd. was done by The Central Canada-Israel

Bank, whose representative wrote to the Custodian General on May 14th, 1953:

"... Mordechai Liebman and Shlomo Zvi Finkelman, file 294.95 in our records, resided, according to our records at the time of sale (March 28th, 1935) at 15 Hillel St., Haifa. It was handled by attorney Shmuel P. Pronman of Haifa (P.O.Box 902). It is not clear from the file whether the buyers paid for the purchase in full, but at our discretion we believe that we should accept the claim made by the buyers and their representative, Attorney Pronman, that the sum was paid in full."

According to the land registration record, ownership of the lot was registered to Mordechai Liebman and Shlomo Zvi Finkelman on March 23rd, 1954. A week later, on April 2nd, 1954 the head of the department at the Land Registry ordered the following comment be added to the file: "Do not carry out any action without approval of the Department Head", and it seems that the Liebman-Finkelman ownership was canceled, following an order by the district court (civil file nos. 668/53 and 17/54). Ownership reverted to the Custodian General, and later in 1997 by another order ownership was transferred to the State, to the ILA. The ILA published a tender for it, which got canceled due to lack of purchase offers.

Didn't my father know that the registration process had been completed and the lot was finally registered to him?

Why was the Liebman-Finkelman ownership of the lot erased and the lot returned to the Custodian General?

Was registration of my father as owner of the lot revoked just because his ID number was not recorded when registering the ownership, combined with the fact that Liebman perished in the Holocaust?

Though I never found unequivocal answers to these questions, Israeli bureaucracy had evidently found a way, as surprising as it may sound and some 58 years late, to return the lot to its legal owners, as declared by the Custodian General already in 1954.

***

The Family, Part II

On March 3rd 2013 my mother passed away, twenty-four days after receiving compensation for the lot. My mother died at the age of 102. On that day, both my sister and I were in the US; I was there for work and my sister was visiting her daughter Shlomit in New Jersey. We returned to Israel immediately and my mother was buried in Haifa on Friday, March 15th.

Nearly four weeks earlier, the day we received payment for the lot, I was sitting with Raya talking about how wonderful I felt that the "journey" to uncover the lot had ended. I said that my father could now rest in peace, or in other words, his spirit could move on.

I am sure that the strange course of events, the goodwill and help I received from everyone, were far beyond the norm. After the dream I had about my father, I found it easier to attribute some of the events to his interference from wherever he might be. I'm fully aware that there is no logical basis for that, but it does reflect how I felt at the time, especially considering the reality of the past year and a half. When Raya replied that my father only needed my mother to join him in order to move on,

I smiled but forgot about it. Only during the shiva did Raya remind me of our conversation.

Today, as I write these lines, I think she was right; I do remember, and I smile.

During the shiva – the Jewish traditional week of mourning – I had occasion to tell and retell my mother's life story – I spoke of her childhood, immigrating to Palestine with my father, their life together until he died, and her old age.

The story of the lot was also told many times during those seven days. Some of my friends had heard bits and pieces over the preceding year-and-a-half and wanted to know how it all ended. Other times the story was my way of responding when I was asked how I knew so much about my parents' early days in Israel and about their families who died in the Holocaust. By the end of the shiva I felt fortunate that the business of the lot had prepared me in a way for my mother's passing. I was so pre-occupied with the distant past, looking over documents and photos, that they tempered the harsh reality and reinforced her image in my mind as she had been all those years ago, at the same time softening to some extent the image of her in old age.

The story of the lot helped me create a memory of my father. My concentrated efforts to look into his actions and investigate his life in the '30s filled a void in my heart. I think and feel that my mother's death also let me say good bye to my father. The story of the lot created an image in my mind with which I could identify and could then form a strong foundation for this final farewell.

***

The Family, Part III

My Aunt Zelda Finkelman-Liebling's bunker diary

My Aunt Zelda's diary was written after she and her husband Joel escaped from the labor camp where they were prisoners. They left their families behind, all of whom were led to their deaths in Belzec. Half of her diary was lost during their liberation, but the other half Zelda brought with her to the US.

Zelda herself translated the diary from Polish to English, and in the interest of authenticity I am refraining from amending it beyond the bare minimum. Later, she would read from it and tell her story to school and university students.

The diary is not only a firsthand account of Zelda's personal tragedy, but also a window into daily life in the bunker, with its emotions, anger and hopes.

January 17, 1944

Finally I got a note-book. After 200 days in the bunker (place of hiding). Who can understand what it means, "BUNKER"; only the one who sits in it knows what it is.

Ever so often, I wonder how should one feel about the person who created a "bunker". Should we bless him or curse him – the future will show. Meanwhile we are sitting and waiting impatiently. Day by day – counting hours – at this moment 4936 hours from the moment we entered here. It was 9:30 pm June 25, 1943 when Lolo and I left the Labor Camp (Lager). It happened suddenly, almost without our doing anything about it. Upon receiving a letter from Hudla – "save your life and I am going to take care of the baby (Lijuchnia)" we ran away from the Lager. The situation was very uncertain for Lolo, because they started taking away dentists, and so we ran like two children without any possessions, like to a ball. It was time to go away (run) but maybe we should have stayed a little longer to find out about my family. At the beginning of being in here I didn't feel or rather didn't understand the mistake we made. Today I feel more and more how foolishly we acted. We went to hide in a bunker – burning bridges behind us. We are still children, or rather completely stupid. Lolo is trying to appease me, who could presume that there'll be a bunker by Rozka and Palanya. I am to blame, because every time Lolo tried to talk to me about hiding I changed the subject. Probably, I thought that the Labor camps would protect us from all evil. What an idiot I was – now it's too late for reproaches, now that Zanka isn't here anymore – there, I wrote the words again – after 7 months I still can't believe it. I live through

that moment the hundredth time and see it vividly –
the morning of the "liquidation"– "aktion". God, if
we ever live to see the "Jeshiya" (freedom) will it be
possible to stop thinking about this? I don't think
so! That macabre scene is still in front of my eyes.
Zanka, my sister – smiling, sits on a stone ready to
die and I am going to live. No, still a few minutes
prior to that. June 23, Wednesday morning. Reveille
at 5 a.m. We all get dressed and something made me
turn around to all the girls in the room and say, "I
have a feeling that this time it is serious." I
embraced my sister Zanka – for the last time in my
life – we kissed and she tried to calm me down –
saying, "well, child, there is nothing we can do –
don't cry" and tears came to her eyes. It was a
bonding moment for both of us. It was unusual of
later days because somehow we weren't together a
lot. This gives me quite a pain now. I remember,
after work (lately we worked separately) we were not
together. I was mostly with Lolo. I know that Zanka
was hurt by it – she never said anything about it, but
didn't hide her feelings. This is why that scene in the
morning means so much to me.

Now we go to the yard where the morning
inspection is taking place. We are immediately
surrounded by a lot of German Gestapo. Lolo tried
to warn us – "go hide anywhere" – but we

disregarded his warning thinking it's just a reveille. When we realized what is taking place Zanka turned around to me and whispered, "You may escape somehow, remember the baby." Oh God, am I going to remember – please God let the child live and I swear to live for her. One more thought is torturing me – when I got up from the ground I just walked away, actually leaving behind me living corpses – I just walked toward life – why didn't I run to Zanka, embrace her, kiss her, maybe it would now be easier to take the pain. Then when they took us to the building, I looked through the window and I saw Zanka sitting down among the others. I even remember watching her urinate in a corner. Somebody came back and told me that Zanka was happy that I was saved, so her little girl is going to have good care. I am sure that Hudla is taking good care of her, better than I ever could. Sometimes I think that maybe I should have pleaded more with those murderers for Zanka's life – but I know how I much I tried – crying on my knees, without getting their attention at all. And still I think that Hudla would have done more.

Tuesday, January 18, 1944

Again, another day passed. There is nothing else to do here but count the days, hours, every day I count anew! We walked in here June 25, and now is January 18. In the other place, the old Czortkow [Chortkow] section, we were hiding for 31 days. That was the time when we were looking around here and we had to run away, while all the others stayed – all the other 8 people. On October 27, the situation became shaky because they found someplace hidden Jews (and killed them), so naturally our hostess became panicky and asked us to leave. Our budget was getting very low, the cold weather on the roof started to bother us, so we left and returned here to the same place. I remember it well as if it was yesterday, though three months passed by since. It was on a Wednesday 2:00 p.m. when we decided to go. We waited for our own guide, Viktor, until 6 p.m.

Wednesday, January 19, 1944

She arrived and we left immediately. A beautiful starlit night, and we (Lolo and I) like lepers – no, worse, two Jews in a "Judenfrei" town (free of Jews) – whoever knows what that means – are walking with pounding hearts, not sure if in a moment somebody would flash a light in our faces. We didn't know how to behave in the streets, how to talk – whisper or speak loud. God, to look down from the hill of the brewery to see the whole city with the light in the windows of the houses; to think that in these houses people live – behind these windows life is going on – one can eat – one can "live" and we are not allowed. We don't exist – just like the "Invisible Couple." And involuntarily the question comes to mind – Why? "Cy bin eich fegn a stein gebojren cy hot mich kein mamy gehat?"– A Jewish saying ("am I born out of a stove or am I not a mother's child?"). And at the same moment, the thoughts are turning the other way – and I have to say myself, but I am alive whereas others are gone.

Further on with reminiscences.... And so we walked with pounding hearts, I even tripped a few times until we arrived finally into this dark, dingy, and hostile place! The bed certainly didn't invite to rest. To make matters worse, the two friends Sara and Hanna right from the start gave us the account of the unpleasant situation in the bunker. Shame, (feh!) such filth among companions in misery. Hearing all that I felt like returning to the other place. For two days I yearned for the pleasant attic – for our quiet solitude. I knew that eventually this situation shall affect us, too. We were drawn into a fight – I am trying to keep calm – saying to myself it's not the worst thing that can happen; and still I get nervous with each quarrel which lasts forever – from petty matters to serious ones. We have here characters! Sometimes I think that living 25 years I didn't encounter as much malice, envy and bad character as much as these people have. They come from all walks of life. The worst one is the refugee from Romania – the scum of the earth – sometimes she likes to play the part of a defender of the working class – the proletariat – but knows about it as much as I know about Islam. Another time she was a hot Zionist. In fact she is a big zero – quarrelsome, maybe somewhere there is a warm heart beating. She fought with everyone already and us too. Well, enough about her, because I think I start sounding like her. Lolo and I call her Yatatayatata – she is close to the nasty character who was the komendant of the Jewish police in the Lager – a former salesman, a real cajoler to our two keepers. Behind the little door he plays his fiddle (behind the little door our two keepers Roska and Palama live, and only men go in there from time to time.) He came to us the latest, paid the most, hates everyone here – and naturally is extremely jealous of his woman, as all old men are. He tries to get her and she plays hard to get. They sleep in the upper bed. In the bottom one, another couple – she is a poor ignorant girl in love with this boy who is using her, he a young fellow who filled his pockets here and is quite pleased with it. The other two beds are occupied by a family – on top the younger brother with his bride, on the bottom the older one, that big fat nothing – characters which could serve as prototypes for Molière's plays. The older brother is like Harpagon – if he could eat again what came out he would be quite satisfied; his beauty is worse. The other day she called me "this lady". I really hate her with a passion. Very often I am ashamed of the company I find myself in. I am trying to persuade myself I am better than others – I am intellectually above them – but it still gets me.

Sometimes I get masochistic about it and think, good for me I deserve this for running away to hide, leaving them all behind. I should have thought about my family, about tomorrow. I should have – Oh God, how often Lolo and I cry about the fact that strangers are here and our families God knows where and what is happening to them. Mama with Lijuchnia, Chaskel and Hudel somewhere looking for shelter while such filth is sitting here in a place that Lolo built for the family. Let's hope it is not too far to liberation day.

Today I cried remembering Lijuchnia standing in the window waiting for us. Oh how it hurts just to think of that beautiful sweet face. This is too painful to write about. Maybe God will help that soon I'll see her and be able to kiss her and hug her. But today's news isn't good, the broadcaster didn't mention Berdyczov or San. So we have to wait for the next broadcast. Our radio news comes from our keeper or her son which I call the Crown Prince. Today our keeper told us the magistrate (town hall) was moved to where the Judenrat was – if that has any political significance. I have to stop writing because I must pay my dues – play cards with the Crown Prince.

January 21

Yesterday I didn't write. I slept most of the day. It was like the first days of our stay here, where to be with Lolo was such a joy. After all the troubles, all the horrible events it was soothing and reassuring to fall asleep next to my husband.

Saturday Jan. 22, 1944

Again a day passed. Today I feel very sad. Every time that guy receives a visitor, his lady-love, I get terribly upset. I dislike him for many reasons. For one, he obstructed our steps to try to get in contact with my family – and here he is receiving an outside visitor who brings him dozens of goodies and also gives some to our keepers. We had an unpleasant situation with them. One of the keepers understood that whatever we have here in the bunker automatically belongs to her. Lolo had here a good quilt and now because our budget was low we wanted to sell it and pay her. Naturally, we were quite surprised to find out about it, and so we must sell the ring Lolo gave me to pay her and be in good standing with her. Now we know why she was angry with us for a while.

It hurts me to find myself in situations like this, but it is all done in order TO LIVE – everything is done just to live, and God will help and we'll have more than we had or just as much. I get very upset about these situations and I think, "How would anybody in my family react to this." Lolo suffers very badly, he looks tired, he lost weight, but he is trying to calm me down and leave these matters to him. Oh, how much longer can I endure this frightful situation; wouldn't it be divine to step outside to breathe fresh air, not that hostile air in the bunker where "homi-homini lupus est." (Man is a wolf to (his fellow) man.)

With all these nasty events I am also depressed because of this morning's dream. As usual, I dreamed of Lijuchnia and Mama. I woke up with a pounding heart and I was sure I called out "Mama." God, will I ever hug and kiss this child and Mama as I do in my dreams. Will I live to see this sunshine of a child – the ray of light which is worth living for after all these tragedies. I still hope to see all of them, but mostly I think of the child. Somehow I feel guilty leaving her and running away from the Lager before I found out what's happening to them. I pray to God not to have a feeling of guilt later on. I love her much more than my own life, and Lolo often says that we feel more love for her than for each other. When I don't sleep I think of them all – how could I not? I know that I have a mother, brother, sister and niece – and don't know where they are, and here I am surrounded by hostile people. It seems that life in a bunker puts its mark on people. One's misfortune doesn't touch the others. Everyone has his cross to bear – everyone went through hell – and one doesn't feel for his fellow man. I myself am carrying my tragedy around with me, and nobody's tears move me. Lolo came back from behind the little door. Coffee time.

January 28, 1944

In a month Lijuchnia will be four years old. I am trying to fool myself that by that time we are going to be free. The broadcasts don't indicate that. The newspapers bring news of big successes of the German armies on the southern front. We were already so close to freedom and again they went back a few dozen kilometers. Sometimes it seems to be a fata morgana (mirage) in the desert – it's close and then it disappears again.

To make matters worse, the winter is the worst. Rain, mud, a winter like never before, the atmosphere in the bunker is unbearable. Only couples talk among themselves. Before we all talked together, we even had a laugh or two; now we have nothing to say to each other. Even among couples there is tension. Lolo is very nervous recently. He has a lot on his mind. Recently a lot has happened. Just Monday Lolo went behind the little door and in a few minutes he came back white as a ghost screaming, "We are lost, Help – fire!" We all thought that somebody saw them and we had been discovered – found out – that means we are as good as dead. Nobody thought of an actual fire. But we already smelled smoke and we got ready to leave. Panic – indescribable. Lolo got the shakes. A few minutes later the old man comes in, the fire is out, and we are saved, thank God. It seems that our keeper kept some gasoline under the bed (in a bottle); when she couldn't see it she lit a match the better to see and so it caught fire and the mattress being made of straw burned very easily. Naturally with the visible flames people from the street came into the house. A miracle that they didn't see our men standing around there, God covered their eyes with his hand. I can see it as an omen – we are going to live and be freed. It would be beautiful to live for Lijuchnia the child and make it up to her for all the miseries.

Every day I reproach myself for burning the bridges behind me, for running away. I acted like a child. I thought that Hudla is going to take care of everything. Now I see how difficult it all must be. If she got in touch with Wisha and gave the child to her and if God helps she is there. How the poor child must feel alone among them, without shoes. I remember when the child was there for two weeks how we brought her home with a dirty head, the voice frightened, and now it's already 7 months – 31 weeks – how does the child live through all that? And still I pray the child should be there because that's her greatest chance to live through all this madness.

The second possibility is that Mama and the child are in hiding someplace and this frightens me for two reasons: security measures and financially. I know that they don't have much money. Even if Leon is with them they still wouldn't have enough. Chaskel and Pepka are someplace, so I heard, and this also worries me, because they are without money. You can lose your mind thinking what could happen. And the situation on the front is, "one step forward and two back." It's hard to see an end to it and we want to live so badly.

Often, when I am in better spirits I dream of the future, making plans with my family. Seeing a beautiful life and my only pain is missing Zanka. Why did she have to go and I remained? What an injustice. She a mother to a child and a much better person than I. How often I see how mean I am. At home they talked me into believing that I am smart – I can't see it, just the opposite – I often act very stupid. Lately there are little misunderstandings between Lolo and myself about minor things. There is now less to eat. Just bread. Only the family has more because of the visitor. Lolo thinks that I am jealous of their good fortune. It isn't that. It's just that I can't stand that "nothing" looking down at me and considering herself something of a better person because she eats better. It hurts for Lolo to think so or to feel that I blame him for having less. If he would only understand. Hudel would understand me, she always did. Lolo is much too touchy. I never pay attention to food, it doesn't bother me at all. I cried, feeling bad that we are treated so badly because of lack of money. We just gave the ring so we have two weeks to go. The watch money is gone. We just have to pray for it to end. The money and everything else is coming to an end.

Monday, January 31, 44

Today we had a very unpleasant situation. The old man lost his watch and we can't find it. We looked everywhere and it is gone. The situation is doubly bad – first of all the finger of suspicion points at any one of us, and secondly our hostess threatened to throw us all out if the watch is not found. That is all we needed to make our misery here worse. I now have such a deep feeling of despair that I would like to break through the walls and run – where to? That is the question. I think that jail is paradise in comparison; at least in jail every page torn out from the calendar means one day closer to freedom. For us it doesn't mean a thing, it's only a day that passed without any meaning or a future. I count days, hours – yesterday was 5,280 hours – 318,800 minutes – this is what I do when I am not asleep. And so, since we are here summer is gone, fall is gone and half of the winter, and we hear the winter is an unusual one – rain and mud and often winds which we hear howling upstairs in the empty rooms. Sometimes it sounds like a faraway shot – the best sound one can hear. Wishful thinking – oh how we would love to hear shooting sounds – cannons or artillery – it would mean so much to us. But nothing; it's much too quiet. The only sound is the whispering of this idiotic couple and the sound of peeling potatoes until it drives you out of your mind. Potatoes – that is our daily menu, but I am still thinking of that watch and what is going to happen to all of us. Somehow, I can see better today, maybe it is lighter. Usually it is much darker in the bunker, because the only light comes from a part of a window – the whole window is covered with board except for twenty cm. On top, the glass is covered with paint so no one can look in from the outside. As bunkers go, ours has enough light, like for pigs – enough for former human beings, which keep alive memories of a better life – that is not enough. I said pigs because this place reminds me of a sty, especially the exit – the trapdoor at the bottom of shelves 40 cm high – that is our connection with the outside world. I am very distracted today – I'll write more tomorrow.

Tuesday, February 1st, 1944

The watch is gone. We didn't find it. It caused a lot of fighting between all 10 people. He suspects everybody and he got our hostess on his side. The atmosphere here is unbearable. I am glad I took hold of myself and I keep quiet like a church mouse. Meanwhile, it is dark today and I can't see. The evening potatoes are ready.

Saturday, February 5th, 1944

Two days of duty kept me occupied and I didn't get a chance to write. This is the time that I can wash myself and my few things. Yesterday we had very bad news – they caught four Jews in a village. It seems that they still hunt those running in fear. I thought that they forgot us – that after seven months of "Judenfrei" they let the case rest. We thought that with the front nearing – slowly maybe but still advancing – those gentiles will have a heart and stop pointing out the Jews to the murderers – but no, this matter never rests, it seems that the Almighty doesn't want us anymore. Just to think – people are suffering for such a long time and when they think that salvation – freedom – is near, that salvation is coming – that's when the worst happens. How terrible it must be to be discovered by the Nazis – what does one go through in those moments of looking them in the face? I saw people going to their death. I saw Zanka, how indifferent she was – almost calm. Most probably facing death one becomes indifferent and loses the will to live. I remember lying on the ground expecting to be shot soon, I saw Lolo fighting for my life – I was just very calm. Now, sitting here, I think of it ever so often. Today I was thinking of all of them and especially Lijuchnia.

God, I'd rather be dead than be left alone. I dreamed of Lijuchnia last night – she was in Zanka's arms – smiling with rosy cheeks – in one moment she was trying to get away from a German officer pleading "Ich will nicht" ["I don't want"]– and so Zanka and I got her out of his hands. Then I saw her among horses and I interpreted it as a good sign – she is among friends. As far as Lijuchnia is concerned I became a great believer. Since I've been here I believe in God more than ever – every night I say a pray for Lijuchnia, God should watch over her. I think it's very natural for people with little hope to turn to religion for support. I always believed – my religion was implanted in me from childhood on, so now after all these experiences it became stronger. Though looking around me I often want to cry out in blasphemy and ask: if God exists how could He look on – see all these horrors, let these murderers do their killing? How could He be so indifferent to all that? But then I pray and ask Him for forgiveness and pray for the safety of my dearest ones.

Except for bad news about the four Jews, we still have the case of the missing watch. The situation is unpleasant but at least our hostess got over it and she is okay. Good, we must be grateful for that. Today she brought her nephew into the bunker to show him how these creatures who were once people live. Crawling in she said, "I could never live like this, I would choke to death." She looks at this from the heights of freedom. She is a human being, we are nothing – less. Sure she wouldn't sleep in a hole where each one of us has 80 square cm to live and the air is coming through a chimney in which the basin [toilet] is for us to use. This thing is very shaky – and quite often overturns. And then I am ready to die because the smell is unbearable and everybody is putting the still-sensitive nose under the cover – and only the poor doer has to clean up the mess. Every time I walk out of the chimney ("the toilet room") I think of what could take place and I shiver at the possibility. That stench is just awful. But that isn't the only one – there is another one just as bad. Right in the middle of the "room" there is a pail for slops (dishwater) everything goes into this pail – it sometimes even serves as a substitute for the chimney if the other one gets too full and can't be taken out. In seven months those pails weren't dry for one second. Nobody washed it because who would put a hand into it, but if a spoon or fork falls into it – it's taken out – just slightly rinsed – and used again. Slightly rinsed because water is scarce. There is one little pail to wash the floor 2 square m. of it – this we do with water from washing ourselves. The pail in the chimney is covered with a rag to diminish the stench. Ha ha – this rag is always wet and smells worse. To make the air heavier, somebody relieves himself from time to time from wind produced by eating those dry potatoes. That's enough about those sensitive noses. The other plague is the tremendous amount of bed bugs which are everywhere and also lice. These bother me most because a bite from a louse leaves me with a rash for quite a while.

Sunday, February 6th, 1944

The days are getting longer – 6 am in the morning is bright and 4 pm it gets dark. I can't sleep and wait for the morning light to start the day. Actually what for – the days are like ages, and to live through one is very hard. So many thoughts run through my head in these 18 hours a day, because again and again I live through the macabre scenes. Today we discussed the final liquidation of the camp with its death. And naturally I thought of Zanka and I saw a grave full of other bodies and again the reproaches came back to me, why did I let her go by herself, why didn't I stay with her. Maybe it's easier to go to death with someone dear beside you. She went to the truck holding Libcha's arm (our cousin). I can still see the open truck with a chair in front of it for everyone to step on it in order to get into the truck. What perfidy! They take people to slaughter but they give them a chair to make it easier to step into the truck – that's "western culture" humanity. I could scream – howl from pain – call to heaven for revenge. Until the liquidation I didn't know so much hatred – such strong desire for revenge. I swear I am going to instill upon Lijuchnia hate for all that's German. Maybe Mel is going to come home, please God, and he'll avenge Zanka's death. But with all that, we'll never get Zanka back, and the wound is never going to heal. I remember the little girl who jumped on the truck. She lost her mother before (they shot her before the liquidation) and the Aryan who kept her didn't want her anymore and brought her back to the labor camp from which they were now taking her to be shot. I keep on thinking how this little girl was going to meet death completely unaware of what's going on. I connect her with the phrase which was said to us by our hostess, "do I have to take off my little chemise too?" The Aryans are repeating this question among themselves with sorrow, now how can we take it! I can't stop thinking about it. I must admit that no death is more painful than a child's. It's such an innocent being – so little, it didn't have a chance to live – it didn't harm anybody – so why does it have to die? You just can't think about it. It's a typical slaughter of the innocent. I hope that the blood of these innocent ones shall fall on their and their children's heads – amen. This doesn't ease the pain at all. God, please spare Lijuchnia! Let me be able to be with her. I think I sinned, so please God forgive me and let me sacrifice [myself] for her. The days go by so slowly. Yesterday we had a good news broadcast.

This is where the diary ends.

Zelda Finkelman-Liebling was born on March 24th, 1918 in Chortkow to Eli and Lifka Finkelman. She studied at the Polish high school and graduated from teachers college in Lvov on the day the German bombing started. She married Joel (Lolo) Liebling and the two survived the war together. They were liberated on March 24th, 1944.

They were the only survivors from their respective families. Lijuchnia did not survive.

They had two children in the US, Mordechai and Linette.

Joel passed away in 1988, Zelda in 1998, may they rest in peace.

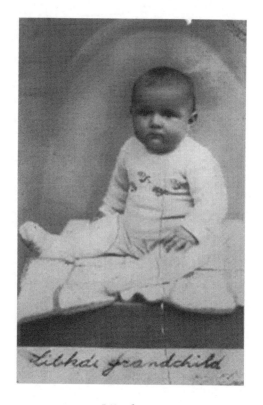

Lijuchnia

***

Testimony

It is rare to find memoirs of a Ukrainian who was a boy at the time and a witness to the extermination of Chortkow's Jews. Despite the fact that this short account was written after the fact and was undoubtedly edited to be "politically correct", or perhaps because it was, the anti-Semitism that was prevalent at the time is so glaring. In just one page Jan's account summarizes the fate and end of Chortkow's Jewish community.

Jan Kruczkowski, a Polish boy from Chortkow who lived near Jews tells of this period:

"The Jews had completely taken over our town. It was hard to compete with them in commerce. They had small stores and large warehouses. The owned both grand houses and seedy ones. They got rich slowly but methodically. They lived in the center of town and were incredibly organized. They had schools, sports teams, synagogues and even an athletics club called Hashmonaim. The poorer neighborhood – the slum – was also in the center of town and later the Germans turned it into a ghetto. I would often see how Jews would do business and bargain. They would haggle aggressively and would praise their wares for hours. It was difficult to get out of there without buying anything. Often people would buy something just so they could leave the store and the annoying, pushy salesman. The Poles, I'm afraid, did not have that talent. Jews also took over transit. They had buses, wagons for their wares and carriages for people. Those carriages were needed by the people of Chortkow because the town sprawls over a large area and has an uneven topography with many hills.

I had daily contact with Jews. I walked with them to school, and often we would play together, but mostly we would fight. I sometimes threw rocks at their miserable houses, especially on the Sabbath and Jewish holidays. I never passed up a chance to pull the payot of spoiled Jewish boys from rich families.

I lived surrounded by Jews. On one side were the Weissmans, on the other side of the yard were the Eisenbaums and their fat son Czesho who was my age, and across the street were the Pifers who had a store. My mother had a good friend – Trenia Golombioska. She always had poor people living at her place. Srul lived there, a little boy with a runny nose, and his older brother Moshko.

To this day I can smell the sweet onions, the stale lard, and the stench of the garbage that was ever present in their house.

I remember Srul who would look at me with hungry eyes whenever I brought candy.

In 1942 they created a ghetto in the center of town for thousands of Jews which was completely sealed off from the outside. They gathered all the Jews from Chortkow and the rest of the region. This Jewish quarter was in the center of town and was surrounded by a barbed wire fence. They used concrete to block the exits, windows and doors that faced the Arian side. At the entrances and exits to the ghetto they posted the Jewish and Ukrainian militiamen.

At first the Jews could still leave the ghetto to visit the gentiles they were friends with, tell them all about the horrible conditions in the ghetto and the cruelty of the militia. They would tell that even among themselves there were fights for survival. The strong took advantage of the weak, the rich ignored the poor; gone was Jewish solidarity. Fear of death took over and stifled any feelings of honor and justice.

I'm afraid the same things happened among the Polish people. Often they didn't want to help, and wouldn't give even a slice of bread. They would shoo away from their doorstep Jewish kids who came begging. Luckily there weren't many of them, but sometimes you just had to say no.

I remember, when the ghetto was being liquidated, a Jewish man we knew came over, an old neighbor from Kolyoba Street, and begged us to save his life. We refused. Our situation didn't allow us to hide him. We lived on a main street that saw a lot of traffic and was open to all. We had a large family and my parents couldn't risk everyone's lives in order to hide a Jew. Did our wretched neighbor understand our situation? He left a fur with us, and never came back for it... for a long time I could not let go of the image of the wretched man who begged for his life. Unfortunately, his Jewish looks left him with no chance of surviving.

The summer of 1942 saw the first Aktion. I saw Jews led in groups of four along Kolyoba Street towards the train station where train cars were waiting for them. In the first row were Rabbis and older men in their traditional clothes, long beards and payot. Sometimes younger men helped support them. They prayed loudly and wailed. It was a horrific sight. I saw them all: Czesho Eisenbaum with his parents, Pifer (who had a store) with their son who was a friend of mine from school, and old Wasserman. When they passed by the house they waved and shouted. I guess they were saying goodbye. We stood at the window and didn't know what to do, how to act. Fear of the thugs stopped me from getting closer to neighbors and acquaintances even though we all knew they were walking to their death."

Based on the Polish-to-Hebrew by Yehudit Shifris (as published on chortkov.org)

***

Memories

I assume that in most families of second-generation Holocaust survivors, or those who managed to reach Palestine before the Holocaust, there lurks an untold story.

The first half of the 20th century was a tumultuous period, full of awful tragedies, expectations, new beginnings, the budding of new life, hope and disappointments. Most of us learned to live alongside the collective family memories with their emotion-laden silence. We picked that up from our parents, some of whom were experts in suppression and concealment. Many viewed memories as a weakness, something tying them to a trauma from which they wished to escape for good. Dealing with memories was tantamount to entering a danger zone, where they would have had to cope again with a personal trauma that had required all their energy to distance themselves from, so that they could lead a normal life. Those who led their lives in the shadows of Memory Lane often became depressed. But most welcomed the challenges of life in a new country as a chance to ignore the past, if not by obliterating the memories then at least by not talking about them with their offspring. Like many of my generation, I was born into that way of life .

The past was not spoken of in our home. Perhaps they also wanted to shelter me from the knowledge of evil.

Not only the memories were hidden, so were the photos. The cardboard shoeboxes and yellowing envelopes containing old photos were a mystery to me. Many Holocaust survivors and early settlers kept old photos: of their families, friends, and the places they came from. Those pictures were kept in envelopes and shoeboxes, never organized in photo-albums. Only once these people had children did they start placing the new pictures in albums. It was as if the old history was locked away, hidden and erased from memory, or at least downplayed, stashed away, isolated from everyday life, while the new life was deemed worthy of preserving as new memories. For all I knew, maybe they did sometimes look at the old photos, but if so, it was done secretively, far from our inquisitive eyes, on nights when sleeplessness reigned. It's an amazing yet common phenomenon: many of us, after our parents' demise, found a veritable treasure of old photos, at least some of which were a mystery to us: Who were these people? How were they related to us? Where do they belong in this memory puzzle? I believe that, whether consciously or not, these pictures were kept hidden away in order to avoid questions, fearing that answers to those questions would stir memories and feelings that were too difficult to cope with.

My gaze into the past is like gazing through fog. That insight came to me during my trip with my wife to Acadia National Park in the US. At that point in time I'd just received the memoirs of Tonia Sternberg – Pepe Kramer's friend – possibly the only witness to the murder of my mother's family. One morning, Raya and I went out on a boat tour among the inlets and islands along the shoreline of Acadia National Park in Maine. That day, sailing conditions seemed adverse initially: a thick fog enveloped the water, strangling the seascape under its gray blanket, and we couldn't see much. But gradually, we got used to the grayness, heard sounds and voices through the fog, and glimpsed sights that emerged from the mist: a fishing boat pulling up its crab net; a buoy with its cylindrical head facing skyward, topped with a red bell, its clanging monotone sounding to the rhythm of the waves, warning of an approaching collision. From time to time the shape of a lighthouse emerged through the thick fog indicating a new shoreline, a relic of days gone by when this was a busy water way frequented by ships. Much later, Raya told me sailing through the fog felt like an enchanted voyage. The fog alternately revealed and concealed the secrets of the place, creating tension between the observable and the hidden, and the feeling that the landscape was not to be taken at face value   Throughout this half-day voyage we didn't see the entire shoreline, nor an uninterrupted view from one horizon to the other, even once. Nonetheless we did not feel as if we were missing anything, but rather it felt like a voyage among sights and sounds that told the story of a place. This experience helped me explain and define to myself my feelings about uncovering my family's past: a type of looking through mists where the visible is only a fraction of the picture, most of which is hidden; but the light flickering through the haze enabled me to paint a picture of my family and connect with hitherto unknown memories of a past long gone. I managed to feel a longing for my father, whom I'd erased from my memory years ago – or so I thought. And suddenly he was back.

My father had been replaced by a picture on the wall. My father died on December 21, 1958. The Hebrew date was the 10th of Tevet [5719]. That's why I hated Israel's national poet, Haim Nachman Bialik, who was born on the same Hebrew day (though in 1873). Every year, when my school held its annual Bialik festivities for the poet, celebrating his birth, I would secretly weep for my father's death.

Whenever our homeroom teacher wrote that date in chalk on the blackboard, I'd brace myself for the question: "Children, who was born on this day, years ago?" Though no one in class knew the answer better than I, I never bothered to raise my hand or call out the answer: I was too busy mourning my father. Years later, the emphasis on the 10th of Tevet was shifted to other memorials: the day of remembrance for all Holocaust victims whose burial place is unknown; and the fast of Tevet commemorating the beginning of the siege on Jerusalem laid by Nebuchadnezzar II and ending with the destruction of the First Temple by the Babylonians. As a child, I thought that those events were more suitable to commemorate my father's death. Today, looking back, I wonder how come he died on one of the two days on which he used to pay his respects to the memory of his murdered family – Yom Kippur (the Day of Atonement) and the general day of remembrance.

I was raised in a secular home. My parents celebrated Jewish holidays, but as a rule didn't attend synagogue services. Once a year only, on Yom Kippur, my father used to go to synagogue, to take part in the Yizkor prayer in memory of his family and friends. My mother kept score with God for not having prevented the murder of her family, and chose to pay her respects to their memory at home. My parents used to light a yahrzeit (memorial) candle every Yom Kippur and 10th of Tevet.

It did not rain in December 1958 – it was a drought year. On a Sunday night, a cool but cloudless evening, my father died. He died suddenly, at home, following a heart attack. Only a wall stood between me, and my father with my weeping mother. Within a short while I was sent upstairs to our neighbors, the Rothsteins. I was told briefly that Father wasn't feeling well and that everything will be all right. But apparently it was not all right. The following morning I was sent to "aunt" Rachel, a close friend of my mother's, where I stayed another day. I was told that my father was unwell, my mother took him to the hospital but he couldn't have visitors. My father's funeral was held on that day. While I was playing Monopoly with imaginary friends, my father was being laid to rest. The next morning I was sent back to school, without a word of explanation. I guess a second-grader shouldn't miss school, certainly not for two days running... My time in school was brief: already at the morning assembly a kid came up to me and asked whether I was the one whose dad died the other day. My reaction was swift and hard: I punched him in the face. I don't think I was punished for it, but the truth quickly sank in.

The looks of the other school kids left no doubt: my father was dead. On my way home, I was greeted by the obituary notices pasted on the pillars at the entrance to the building. I think I've never tried to visually recall those seven days of mourning. But today, through the mists of time, I vaguely recall an image of myself entering our home. My mother, pale and puffy-eyed, surrounded by her women friends. My sister, sitting in a corner, watching me, dazed. And as if in slow-motion, they both got up and walked over to me. I don't remember much crying, neither mine nor my sister's. I think I felt a dissociation, which accompanied me all my life. No one ever spoke to me of, nor discussed with me, my father's death. He just died one day, left our lives, to be replaced by a picture on the wall.

I never said goodbye to my father. Over the years, very gradually, my childhood memories of him faded until they disintegrated completely. Only his picture on the wall over my mother's bed continued to stare at me for years, until the day I noticed that the photo had been changing, getting younger with each passing year.

Memories should be nurtured. That's the only way to preserve them. And nurturing them is done through a story that breathes life and validity into them. You relate the memories, and they return the favor by growing stronger and finding a safe, permanent spot in your consciousness, until they become part of you. That's how the story of going fishing with Father evolved into the nearly sole memory of my childhood; a live memory that lets me describe details in the most amazing clarity: My father's clothes, down to the last detail; the clothes his friends Grave, Grossman and Israel wore; the minutiae of the decrepit balcony of the one-story cement building from which we fished; the slippery rock I climbed onto, the better to cast the bait into the water; the way the fish looked and smelled, and the salty smell of the water. I caught thirteen fish, whereas they, the expert fishermen, didn't catch a single one. No wonder this was the memory I chose to nurture – memories of a proud kid. For years I'd see those images in front of my eyes at bedtime, during school, during hard times, and times when I thought of my father. Moments when I suddenly missed him, or just out of the blue, for no apparent reason. Over the years, I gathered facts about my father's life. He seemed to me a man who made his dreams come true until his dream was cut short. According to others', he was the persevering type, a man who tenaciously strove to reach his goal, who felt compelled to reach the targets he set for himself. That's what drove him to leave Chortkow for Vienna to study engineering and architecture. That's how he decided to immigrate to Palestine. That's why he didn't give up but continued to court my mother despite her parents' objection and returned to Europe to propose to her and marry her. That caused him to insist on leaving Poland, with my mother and her sister, when WWII broke out, brought them to Palestine, saving their lives. And that was the motivating force behind his decision to quit working as an architect and switch to a career of a philatelist, converting his hobby into a profession that would provide my family with an income for a long time after he passed away. Though I always drank in every word when people spoke of my father, still I could not create a complete picture of him in my mind. Perhaps because, over the years, my mother stopped talking about him. My sister never talked about him, and our relatives kept their comments to occasional observations such as "You're so much like him..." or "You have the same personality." Such comments begged more questions, aroused my curiosity; but they were never accompanied by any substantial story that could add details to his character, paint him as a real figure rather than one becoming increasingly vaguer to me with time.

My father's home at 279 Szpitalna, Chortkow

And suddenly he was back. The story of the lot brought my father's memory back from oblivion. During the year of my quest I kept thinking that I was looking not only for the lot in this puzzle but for my father's story, and with it, the story of the family I never got to know.

I got to know my father's assertiveness, and to marvel at his command of the Hebrew language and his beautiful penmanship in the new language he learned in his youth, before coming to Palestine. The search for information related to the forgotten lot managed to create a new memory. The missing details were completed by fragmented facts and the process of discovery itself, which, combined, created a new experience, a kind of collective memory of the family and the era. This patchwork memory enabled me to learn not only about my father and my family but also about the town of Chortkow and its fate.

During my entire youth there were but two cases where the wall of silence cracked just enough for me to peek into my parents' "Chortkowian" past. In both cases it had to do with books. First, there was The Chortkow Book – a book commemorating the Chortkow community, edited by Dr. Yeshayahu Austri-Dunn published in 1967. The second was "Af Echad, Af Echad Lo Ohev" – "No one, no one loves" by Ora Shem-Or, published in 1969. The two books are quite different. The first is the impressive work of the so-called Book Committee of the Chortkow Association, and funded by them; the second is a collection of short stories by Israeli writer Ora Shem-Or, née Sonnenschein, originally of Chortkow.

After the Six Day War (1967), when I was about sixteen, as I came home after being to the movies with friends – I recall it was You Only Live Twice with Sean Connery – my mother handed me a heavy tome, saying: "This is the Chortkow book. Read it and look after it. It tells about your father." I remember not sleeping a wink that night. The book told it all, not just about my father. About the

Chortkow of long ago, history, stories, tales, memoirs – and, inter alia, about Father and his family. First I leafed through, looking for pictures of familiar faces. Then I read. Then I browsed through, then read it again, avidly drinking in every word. This was my first real glimpse into my family's past, a world unto itself that, until that moment, had been locked away and inaccessible to me.

The following day, my eyes bloodshot from lack of sleep, my mother's probably from crying, I was finally introduced to the box of photos. In our case it wasn't a cardboard shoebox but a beautiful wooden box made by Father in 1934. It held a jumble of assorted old photos, postcards and letters. Pictures of my parents, of my family that is no more, a family exterminated in the Holocaust. Everyday pictures of bathing in a stream, a family outing; pictures taken at Zionist youth movements, pictures of parents and their newly-married offspring; and pictures of my parents and sister on their last visit with the family in Chortkow, on the eve of the war. That's when I first heard the story of that visit and the statement "We could have saved them… or at least taken Moshe, my kid brother, with us… we didn't know that Heaven could turn into Hell in one day." A few short sentences embodying all my mother's guilt feelings – the only survivor of the Kramer family.

I know now that, as a kid, I had no idea how to handle this newly-acquired knowledge. Though I took in every written word, and scanned to memory and mind every single picture, I let this discovery get pushed back and forgotten. As I closed the lid of that box, I put the lid on those memories for many years. Maybe because I found it hard to see my mother suffering, when I realized how difficult it was for her to speak of the past. Or maybe because it was all so inextricably entwined with the memories of my father, a memory I was busy repressing.

On one of my weekends off from Hadassim, my boarding school, when I was a senior, aged eighteen, I came home in the afternoon, and was witness to a heated phone conversation between my mother and her best friend Lola (Leah Pevzner.) That was the first time I heard my mother swear in Polish, on the phone, "psha kref cholera" (Polish spelling: psia krew cholera; meaning loosely "may you be struck with cholera!"). This curse was reserved for situations of extreme distress, such as when someone snatched victory from her at the Friday night card game. This was strange because Lola was not among her card-playing circle. To me she seemed like my mom's intellectual younger friend, with whom she discussed Life, Literature and Theater. My mother held her in high esteem. I quickly found out that this colorful curse was my mother's spontaneous reaction to Lola's quote from Ora Shem-Or's book jacket blurb: "Weren't there any normal people in Chortkow? Were they all twisted, corrupt, troubled, disturbed? If there were – the author didn't know them. These brief encounters with the protagonists will shock the readers and shake them up, from deep sorrow to hysterical laughter. The book will affect the Israeli reader the way Peyton Place affected the American reader." Even though the author wrote a cynical disclaimer on the first page, to the effect that "any resemblance between the characters in the book and the people living in Chortkow during my childhood are the product of my weak memory and deceptive imagination," the blurb had hit hard, offending Chortkow pride. To my mother and her friends, this was a type of malicious slander of the memory of people and a community that had been exterminated. "You do not make fun of the dead... she is a bad woman... her family never loved her..." From that moment on, Mother forgot how much she enjoyed Shem-Or's newspaper articles and her column in La'Isha, the popular Israeli women's magazine.

And, from that day on, I was treated to unprecedented openness on my mother's part on the subject of her family life in Chortkow. "They were nothing like she describes... I'm not saying there weren't any bad or crazy people there; Chortkow was a normal place, with people of all sorts. But to say they were all abnormal and disturbed? That's just being nasty ... My parents were really good people, righteous even. My parents brought up three orphans before they had children of their own. They always preferred the orphans to us. They knew it was hard on me, but explained that the orphans had no parents, so they had to compensate... On Fridays I'd go with my father to hand out challahs and food to the needy; is that nasty?! Father was a gabbai (beadle) at the synagogue, he always helped the needy, is that nastiness?!" For hours, she told me about her home, her daily life as a young girl, her girlfriends, school life, the friend in New York with whom she corresponded for years, whose name was also Lola. As far as I recall, Lola sat next to my mom in high-school. I actually met Lola in 1980, on my first trip to a professional conference in Mexico, when I stayed overnight in Manhattan. On impulse, without prior planning, I opened a Manhattan phone book, found her name, called, and invited myself over for tea and rugelach (chocolate-filled yeast pastries) that she baked for me. Her home was just a couple of blocks away from my hotel. I remember nothing of that encounter except the phrase "Ronny, you look so much like Junio."

To my great chagrin, at eighteen I wasn't wise enough, nor sensitive, strong, brave nor mature enough to take the opportunity to ask more questions, questions that I didn't know could be asked, questions I want to ask today, but there's no one left to ask.

Within the shoebox, in the dark, the memories are safely locked. Outside of the box, the memories live on, breathe, keep changing. Yesterday's memory is unlike today's, and definitely unlike tomorrow's. Within the shoebox, time has stood still, frozen. As if waiting for someone to remove the lid, let the light and fresh air in, breathe life into them and create new memories.

The tale of the lot removed the lid from the box. This time, I was ready to face the memories.

***

Viktor

"Why don't you go there?" my colleague Uri asked me one morning at work. Hanan joined in with the suggestion "It can add another dimension to your story." Almost immediately I replied that my story is virtual, I don't need to go anywhere to write it. "The story came to me, I did not go to it" I answered with a sort of wisecrack.

My mother always referred to Chortkow as "that goddamned place". "The ground is soaked with blood... it is one giant cemetery," she would reply when I tried to convince her we should visit her hometown. The last time I brought it up was in the early nineties after the USSR dissolved, while she was living in an assisted living home in Tel Aviv. We believed, Ilana and I, that this was the last chance before she was no longer able to make the trip to her hometown. The three of us sat on a bench in the garden and I entreated and Ilana lent her support. My mother's response was decisively final: "There is nothing for me there, no acquaintances, no friends, no memories, no family, only blood and bones and graves."

Uri's question kept reverberating in my head and wouldn't let me be. Doubtless my mother's words were etched into my consciousness and could not be erased. But on the other hand, I was always drawn to visit Chortkow. Many times I would ponder the words "grieve by a grave", and did not understand why it was okay to visit the graves of parents, family, and friends but it was impossible to visit Chortkow. After all, it was also a place of happy childhood memories, friendships, and love. Perhaps it was the killing and hatred, or perhaps guilt was the real barrier. I never got a proper answer from my mother. I believed it was her inability to face the memories, to let the past into the present.

These thoughts would not let go. I kept thinking of Uri's question on the drive home, and while on the elliptical at the gym, I felt that my response to his question was not quite accurate. I wanted to travel towards the past but didn't know in what way. I knew what I didn't want, but had only an inkling of what I did want. I didn't want to travel with other people. I didn't want to share collective memory or sorrow. I wanted to see Chortkow through my own eyes, or, more precisely, my camera's lens. I knew that many second-generation Chortkow survivors had visited the town in recent years and might visit again in the near future, but I felt that wasn't the trip for me. As I kept exercising, the kind of experience I was looking for came into focus. I knew I wanted to be alone. I knew I wanted to take photos. To see the houses where my family lived, where my parents grew up. To walk the streets and paths they walked. To feel the place where my family lived many years ago. To get to know the landscape, the Seret River, the ruins of the castle above the town, the surrounding villages. I knew many things would move me, but I did not think it would be a trying experience.

I needed to find a local guide who spoke English. From conversations with those who had visited Chortkow I knew none of the locals spoke English. Most visitors used a guide who was not a local resident, but spoke English and could act as a go-between, translate and make them feel comfortable. That wasn't enough from me. I wanted a local. Someone who was born in Chortkow, who spent his childhood in the town where my parents were born, a man who was emotionally attached to it and knew every hidden spot. If he was interested in photography, so much the better, we could indulge in our hobby together. Honestly, though, I did not believe I could find someone who would fulfill such detailed demands.

Despite my doubts I embarked on my search with gusto. I knew the only way to look would be online. A search for "tourist guide in Chortkow" didn't yield any results. I spent hours at the computer, and the best I could find were tour guides from Lviv – 200 km from Chortkow. I felt that wasn't good enough. I needed a local, or there was no point in going.

On Friday night, as sleep eluded me, I felt the cogwheels of my mind spinning. If I was looking for a local, I reasoned, it would be best to search for "West Ukraine tour guide born in Chortkow", and with that in mind I finally fell asleep. Naturally, when I awoke the next day I didn't remember anything, but after a few more hours of random web searching it hit me. "This is sure to work" I thought, though I had no rational reason to believe so. I typed into Google "tour guide born in the city of Chortkow in Western Ukraine". And that's how I found Viktor.

I browsed Viktor's website, which had eluded me until then, reading all the detailed information, I started laughing out loud. It was as though someone had listened to my wishes and created the perfect match: a tour guide in Western Ukraine, with a car and driving license, born in Chortkow, currently living in Ternopil – the Provincial capital located only 70 km from Chortkow, about an hour's drive. Viktor grew up in Chortkow, studied business administration, grew bored with office work, volunteered for UNIFIL and served for a year in the peace keeping force in Lebanon. During this time he also visited Syria and Israel. After about a year, he moved to Ireland, where he lived for ten years. Viktor says on his website that he is an amateur photographer and offers to lend photography equipment to tourists who hire him as a guide. In that moment I knew two things: I'm going to Chortkow, and Viktor will be my guide. Two photos taken by Viktor, which I found on a photography website – a landscape with a blue church on a cloudy day, and a photo of a damaged headstone in an abandoned Jewish cemetery – sealed the deal.

I immediately sent Viktor a detailed email. I introduced myself and told him my parents were born in Chortkow but left before World War II. I told him that practically their whole family in Chortkow perished in the Holocaust and that I wanted to visit. That I wanted to get to know the town, and, if possible, identify their old homes and the gravesites of previous generations, as well as see the places where my parents and their friends spent their time when they were young, and hopefully connect with the place. I wanted to visit the nearby villages and towns: Jagielnica, Yazlovets and Buchach, travel along the Seret River and see the nearby castles. Viktor promptly replied: "I'm thrilled to have the opportunity to show you the town where

I grew up... I've never done that before... I'd have to prepare." Could it be that showing a tourist around his hometown would be emotionally charged for Viktor, too? How do the locals feel about the fact that a third of the town's population was killed in the Holocaust? It never occurred to me that his family, or his friends' families, might be living in houses that used to belong to Jews. Perhaps even my own family's house. Would that be a problem? Raya helped me snap out of it with her direct response: "Does it bother anyone in Israel that we live on Arab lands or even in abandoned Arab homes? Do we care about the dozens of Arab villages that were wiped out and are no longer remembered? If it doesn't bother us, why would it bother them?" Raya's comparison helped me set my head straight: I am going for the experience, not pass judgement. The visit might evoke all kinds of emotions, but they will be part of the experience. I liked the idea of sharing that experience with a local, a third generation of the Holocaust.

I told Viktor I'd like to plan the visit for mid-August 2013. I wanted to go for a week and stay in Chortkow for most of the trip. Viktor replied that he was available and suggested we meet at the Lviv airport on the 18th. I confirmed and ordered my plane ticket right away. Viktor suggested that on the day I arrive we travel from Lviv (Lvov) to Ternopil (Ternopol), see a few medieval castles, stay over at his place and plan the rest of the trip the following day. I agreed. Not making any plans in advance suited me just fine. I wanted to play it by ear and only plan from one day to the next. I didn't want the trip to be too rigid. I didn't want to feel like I had to do anything or stick to a schedule. I believed that the trip would set its own pace.

A few days later Viktor emailed me again and asked that I send my family's addresses in Chortkow so he could look up any other relevant information, should any such information still exist after so many years. He also informed me that he was working to gain entry and the key to the two local synagogues. He told me that they are no longer active synagogues – one is used for various activities and the other is an abandoned warehouse. Viktor commented that it was good that our meeting was a month away because it gave him time to trace any information available about my family. Truth be told, I did not believe he would be able to find anything of significance, as most of the locals from that period had passed away. Many of the old archives were damaged or destroyed, and large portions of the archives are probably kept under wraps by the government for any number of reasons, from protection of property (Ukraine doesn't have an agreement with Israel regarding the return of Holocaust victims' property) to protecting old-timers, including leaders.

Deep inside I knew this was only the beginning. After the events of the past year-and-a-half, I was sure that the mere decision to visit Chortkow and choosing Viktor as my guide would bring with it new discoveries – or so I hoped.

I did not expect the first discovery to come so fast. Saturday morning, while still in bed checking email on my iPhone, I saw a message from Viktor:

"A few years ago a hidden treasure was found in your parents' basement. I know the man who found it but haven't spoken to him yet. It's possible that the government confiscated most of it. It contained paintings and silver... I'm attaching pictures of rooms at the hotel in Chortkow and a picture I took of your parents' house."

The picture was of the Kramer family home, the house where they lived on Sobieskiego St. from which they were forced out by the Soviets in 1939. Later that day I got another email: "I will talk to the man who found the treasure, he has more information. I don't know where the treasure is, but maybe we'll find out together."

How could anyone simply go on with their day after such a revelation? I thought that, by now, nothing could surprise me anymore in this saga, but I was wrong. Events have their own dynamic, and one thing begets another. Once a door has been opened, or a connection made, events unfold of their own accord. A few days ago there was no Viktor, no trip to Chortkow, and now there was a trip, and Viktor, and even a treasure hidden 74 years ago. I wrote to Viktor and thanked him for his hard work and stunning discovery. I let him know I had no wish to claim the treasure, but I would love to photograph the items and hear how they were found. I was worried that the man who had found it might get spooked, break contact and wouldn't meet with me. With the existence of the treasure still echoing in my mind, refusing to leave my consciousness and move into the back, I began preparing for the trip. I put together all the addresses and some pictures of people and houses from those days in a small folder to take with me. I also wrote to Miri Gershoni, asking her to put me in touch with Kobe Kon, that is Jacob Cohen, who was my family's neighbor in Chortkow. Kobe, about fifteen years younger than my parents, was the boy who lived across the street.

A boy who witnessed my family's everyday life. Kobe survived the Holocaust in Chortkow and immortalized my family members in his memoirs.

"Your parents came from different worlds," he told me, "your mother from a Hasidic home, her father from the Stretin Hasidic dynasty and your grandmother wore a wig. I used to go past their large store-and-warehouse every day. Your father, Junio Finkelman, came from an educated family. They belonged to Rabbi Shapira's Synagogue. Rabbi Yeshayahu-Meir Shapira was the first Zionist rabbi in Chortkow. He encouraged his congregation to get an education and convinced parents to encourage their children to pursue post-secondary studies. Your mother's parents opposed their marriage, your father wasn't observant enough... there was no love lost between the rabbis' communities [...] I remember that in the far window was Dr. Karl Halstuch's office, your Aunt Zelda's lawyer husband. In the next window Dr. Simka worked. They lived together. The grandfather died when I was about ten [...] there was another house on their land that they rented out. It was further down and the entrance was in an alley off Szpitalna St. [...] I remember your parents came from Palestine, before the war, to show off their new baby, I remember it like it was yesterday. They managed to get out when the war broke. I met Zelda, your father's sister, and Zigush (Sigmund) her son, after the war when we all came back to Chortkow. Adam, her second son, did not survive. Later they went to stay with your uncle in Colombia. I also met Loushu, your cousin Zelda and her husband Lolo, everyone came to see who and what survived, but found nothing because everyone was dead and everything had been stolen. It was very difficult; it's hard to describe just how difficult [...] I remember we played soccer when I was a little boy. The ball flew into the Finkelmans' yard and I was very scared... I went home to ask my mom to get the ball back... I can still remember how the ball flew into their yard... I don't think it broke anything, but I was scared."

Later in our two-and-a-half-hour meeting with Kobe, he went over a map of Chortkow with Miri and me and pointed out the houses of my near and far relations. I tried my luck and asked if he knew Mordechai Liebman, or anyone else from the Liebman family, but unfortunately he did not. Towards the end of our meeting Kobe turned to me, as though to answer an unasked question:

"You know, through all the years that I've worked and built a life here I never thought of Chortkow, neither I nor my wife who survived Auschwitz.

Maybe we didn't have time for memories. But today, and in recent years, I think about it and remember a lot... so much so that I can't tell if my memories are real or imagined... I remember people, houses and the smallest details... I sit for hours and recall things. I remember how it used to be, not what it's like today. I visited with my son and Miri about five years ago... but the memories and the images are from the past... when I was a boy and youngster."

***

On My Way

Flight PS778 from Tel Aviv to Kiev took about three hours and twenty minutes. I fell asleep shortly after the plane left the gate and taxied to the runway. I don't remember it taking off, I was too busy thinking about the trip on which I was embarking, and those thoughts quickly turned into a dream. I woke up when the flight attendant announced that we were landing and had to fasten our seatbelts. I felt as if I'd jumped ahead in time. I like falling asleep on planes and suddenly finding out the flight is nearly over. When my fellow passenger, Sergei, asked me for the purpose of my trip, as the plane began its descent, I answered with a smile: "A sort of family visit... I'm going to see places, family and friends I don't know yet." Despite Sergei's perplexed look, I felt my answer had been accurate, it wasn't your typical "roots trip". I knew there was no better description for the journey I set out in the early hours of the morning. I had a few goals and questions I wanted answered, but mostly I felt it was a journey into the past, unlike other trips or vacations. I wanted to connect past with present and create new memories of people and of a time that will never return. The layover in Kiev was short. Going through emigration control and moving between terminals kept me focused and cut short my apprehension about the encounter with Chortkow. The first flight's passengers had been a mix – many were Israeli, but the flight from Kiev to Lviv had only Ukrainians aboard. I felt like an alien. The Cyrillic letters and Slavic language, which sounds so foreign to my ears, increased my feeling of alienation. So my first meeting with Viktor was accompanied by a sense of relief. I liked his straightforward attitude. "I suggest that we drive to Ternopil today. It's about a three hour drive, but if we stop at a couple of castles and palaces it'll take us until late afternoon and we'll arrive at my place in the early evening." We loaded my suitcase into the car, I took out my camera and we were on our way. Traffic was light. When I commented on the good quality of the roads Viktor laughed and said this was probably the only road in Ukraine that was up to Western standards, it was paved for the UEFA European Championship and hasn't had a chance to deteriorate yet. Alongside various Western cars, I was surprised at the number of Russian Lada cars, fifteen and twenty years old, some running on gasoline some on natural gas; evidence of a class gap and social polarization. Viktor, as though reading my mind, explained that with a $150 a month salary, which is what the average civil servant makes, it's hard to afford a new car. "All government employees and civil servants take on a second job, each according to their ability and workplace. First, you need enough to live on, and only then do you spend money on luxuries..."

After about an hour's drive we reached Olesko Castle. For a moment it reminded me of the familiar landscapes of Germany or France. A large structure situated on top of a hill, part fortress, part palace. Green fields stretched across the horizon, and tourists in their Sunday best walked hand in hand up the hill. The only difference was the language. It was Polish, Viktor confirmed after I'd recognized my mother's native tongue. The castle was part of a Polish historic route, a kind of heritage trip for Poles who were forced out of Ukraine, or a trip tracing the history of Polish Kings for others. The castle, now serving as a museum, was impressive. It magnificently displayed the 700 years of kingdoms, wars, natural disasters, ruin and rebuilding that it endured. Today it offers tourists its architectural charm and prized works of art.

This was the first time I encountered Ukraine's many beauties: the landscape, the beautiful houses, the palaces, synagogues, gravestones, women... it was such a surprise because the last thing I expected to encounter in this trip was beauty.

Christ - detail of a wood sculpture at Olesko Castle

Pidhirtsi Castle - view from the gardens

Our next stop was an enormous castle – "as though it had been moved intact from its place along the Rhine..." I chuckled to myself as the thought crossed my mind; I was associating its beauty with places I know, but perhaps here were the originals?

This was Pidhirtsi Castle, built in the mid-17th century. Located about 80 km east of Lviv, it was most likely designed by an Italian architect influenced by Muslim, Spanish and North African styles when working on the castle walls. It is surrounded by pleasant gardens and a breath-taking pastoral landscape. The castle was used by Polish kings as a palace and withstood many attacks by great armies who tried to conquer it, such as the Cossacks, the Turks, Austrians, Russians and Germans. In the last decade the castle and palace have stood deserted. They are closed to the public, time and neglect eating away at the walls and buildings till they are in danger of collapse. Viktor explained the situation in Ukraine, comparing it to a grand palace crumbling with time: "Everyone takes for themselves, and no one cares about the whole."

Though by now it had sunk-in that Ukraine had many more beauties to offer than I expected, I was still surprised to see the next place we visited Zolochiv Castle. The palace, spectacular in its character and architectural finesse, replaced the images of the crumbling castle we'd left just an hour earlier. The palace seemed as though it had just been completed yesterday. Its earthy red color suited its delicate shape, and, its position within an open garden, gave it perfect proportions. Undoubtedly, the castle and palace were a surprising aesthetic experience after the neglect we had witnessed at the previous castle. This marvelous castle was built in the 1630s, and the palace added decades later. The castle was conquered by the Turks in the latter half of that century, and came back under Polish rule in the early 18th century. In the 19th century it was sold to the Austrian Empire. The picturesque castle was converted into a hospital, and later a jail. As I walked through the gorgeous gardens at the front, I noticed a sign by the entry gate. In shock, with chills down my spine, I read the sign commemorating 14,000 local Jews who were murdered in the holocaust and 2000 Jewish victims who were murdered in a pogrom by Ukrainian peasants two days after the Germans conquered the region. The Jews murdered on July 4th, 1941 were buried in a mass grave on the castle grounds, right under my feet. It was my first encounter with death in Ukraine. A chilling and unexpected experience in one of the most beautiful and serene places I have ever seen. It was an inconceivable juxtaposition of architecture, culture and art above ground, and thousands of Jewish victims in a mass grave below. A kind of dissonance that couldn't be bridged, a mixture of heaven and hell all in one place. I couldn't contain the contradiction and tears came to my eyes.

Zolochiv Castle

For a long time I was restless. I knew that probably every piece of land in Ukraine, especially in Galicia, bore the scars of hundreds of mass graves. That I could be standing over such a grave, in this pastoral setting, was shocking to me. Neglect and dereliction were what I associated with death. This beauty and aesthetics created an intolerable contradiction.

We continued on our way to Ternopil. At first we were silent, but after a few minutes we began to talk.

I told Viktor that I was done for the day; I had no energy, need, or wish to see anything else along the road. I asked that we stop by a liquor store so we could pick up some cold beers for dinner. I was amazed by the selection of beers and vodka found in a local liquor store, dozens, all for the same price as pop. Clearly, I would sleep well that night. We agreed that, over dinner, I would tell him and his wife Tania why I decided to visit Ukraine. I thought that if I shared the story of the lot and all the events of the past two years it would help Viktor better understand what this trip was all about. Viktor smiled and asked if it was a sad story, I replied that it was both happy and sad. "I think my aim here is to connect to a memory I don't yet have, something I want to discover and experience here."

Viktor took advantage of the last few minutes before we reached his home to be open with me: "Tania might be sad... we lost our baby about two months ago... we came back from Ireland so we could have the baby here and he died after fifteen days." Heavy stuff indeed, and it added to the dark atmosphere that surrounded us since we left Zolochiv Castle. I was apprehensive about meeting Tania, but my fears evaporated as soon as I saw her beautiful smiling face. Tania was happy to see me. I felt welcome. We enjoyed delicious pasta and cold beer, and the conversation flowed. I told them of the lot, and how events unfolded as though guided by a hidden hand just for me. Viktor asked many questions so as to better understand the order of events and the various family relations. He had a hard time understanding the religious and cultural differences between my mother's and father's families; for him all Jews from that period, of which he learned from photos, were the same. I did not find anything offensive in his words, his questions were completely innocent. He was of a generation that learned of local history through the filters of a communist government, to whom religion was superfluous and harmful, and Jewish or any other ethnic history was dangerous. After Ukraine broke away from the USSR it chose not to deal with the horrific memory of the extermination of Jews, in which its residents had taken an active part. Viktor lives in a country where the grand vestiges of Jewish culture are crumbling, synagogues and cemeteries are disappearing and there is no local or national policy to preserve them. What little Viktor knew was from reading and meeting Jewish tourists while guiding them on their roots-tracing tours. But I was the first whose family came from Chortkow; my family's homes were near his home, the story I told took place in his hometown. It wasn't a distant story, it took place right here under his feet, in the air that he breathed. And it raised questions. I think the most difficult issue to deal with was the erasure of memories – the victim doesn't want to remember, so as not to awaken old demons and relive the trauma, and the murderer is too ashamed to tell the story. And so, absurdly, the silence is preserved.

The story I tell sounds like a mystery, or historical romance, where the protagonists fall in love, get separated, reunite, escape from hell, start a family in a faraway land, their families are murdered and their son goes back to the scene of the murder to look for memories – this story creates a kind of shared experience, empathy, something one can identify with. The story builds a bridge and suddenly we are all part of it. You could feel it in the air, in our words, in our looks and even in the way the beer tasted.

Viktor was on board, all excited, and suggested that tomorrow, before we drive to Chortkow, we go into Ternopil and try our luck at the local archives: "There's a good chance you could find documents related to your family." I try to cool his enthusiasm: "I don't believe we'll find anything... many went there before me and couldn't find any documents related to Jews... there's no documentation of anyone being sent to Belzec... people I know were told that the old Chortkow Archives burned down...

and the Belzec Museum also said they had no documents. It's a waste of time." Viktor wouldn't let it go, and I gave in thinking there might still be a chance. Perhaps that guiding force will play a part once again and we will find something of value.

***

At the Archives

I woke up after a good night's sleep. Viktor and Tania's apartment in Ternopil is pretty, modern and spacious. The warmth and coziness of their place made me feel like I was staying with friends. I was amazed that Viktor felt more like a friend than a guide. The conversations of the day before brought us closer, sparked a shared interest and created a joint challenge, and, surprisingly, we became full partners in this adventure. While drinking my first cup of excellent espresso, I suggested Tania join us for the trips outside of Chortkow and got a smile of agreement.

It was a holiday in Ternopil, but not really a day off. Throngs of people in festive white clothes, holding flowers and apples, were gathered around churches. It was the Feast of the Transfiguration, celebrated by Orthodox denominations on August 19th of the Gregorian calendar. According to the gospels, on this day, Jesus received equal status with Moses and Elijah with whom he was seen talking on top of Mount Tabor and heard the voice of God call him "son". The priests' chanting echoed through the speakers. It was their customary Blessing of First Fruits of the year.

The archives were open. It was a vast building that had seen better days. We passed a bored guard at the entrance. The halls were dark and the walls were in dire need of a paint job. A lighter shade would not be amiss at all, I thought, but the most prominent sensation was the stillness. There was no movement in the building and for a moment I thought the employees might be off for the day, or taking part in the praying outside. Viktor led and I followed into the first room. Behind piles of paper and folders sat an elderly clerk who did not raise his head when Viktor asked where we should look. He sent us down the hall to try our luck in one of the other rooms. This time we came across a younger clerk. She lifted her gaze, listened to Viktor's questions and told us to go to room 18 on the top floor. I liked the room number. It stands for good luck in Judaism. Here we met a severe-looking clerk. She had an air of authority. This room was also full of folders and piles of documents on the tables and shelves. It seemed as though nothing had been moved in ages. An old computer, turned off, sat on the corner of a desk, and the smell of old paper filled the air. She listened to Viktor's questions and they talked quietly in Ukrainian. I, of course, didn't understand a word. Suddenly Viktor asked that I write down the names I was interested in, and as though on autopilot I wrote down: Mordechai

Liebman, Dr. Sima Finkelman, and Menachem Mendel Kramer. I could write down more names, but that's what I wrote. Next to each name Viktor added a note in Cyrillic letters and then gestured to a door. I left first and Viktor stayed behind for a few minutes, probably still talking to the clerk. "I believe we will find documents. Tomorrow morning we'll have to come back. I'll ask Tania to come and pick up whatever they find; I believe they'll find documents that did not go up in flames." When Viktor saw the astonishment on my face he added with a smile: "In Ukraine you need to know how to search... the stamps to prove the documents are authentic will cost you a pretty penny...and I explained that you had no problem paying." Again I felt like an actor in someone else's script. This time I was about to find documents. I could feel it clearly. Will I find out who Mordechai Liebman was? Or what happened to my Aunt Sima the doctor? Or any other details about my grandfather Menachem Mendel Kramer and his family? I did not know the answers. One thing I did know: I would have them soon enough.

***

On Route to Chortkow

In the suburbs of Ternopil I saw my first Jewish cemetery in Ukraine. I had no expectations, which is why, perhaps, I found it so full of surprises. The cemetery was situated on a hill overlooking the city, as though the best views and exposures were chosen for its "residents". The gravestones were all cut from local stone and impressive in their design and the craftsmanship they displayed. Some of the symbols on them were unfamiliar to me, being unlike current-day Israeli headstones. The inscriptions were succinct, honoring the deceased and only hinting at the circumstances of death – was it old age or was it unexpected, was it a young man or a maiden. I was quickly able to connect the symbols with the description and sex of the deceased: candles or a candelabra meant a woman, because women bless the candles for the Sabbath; a branch or broken flower indicated an unwed virgin; a tree or an oil jug described a scholar; a star of David for a man; hands held for the priestly blessing of a Cohen. Beautiful headstones, each telling a story, with the inscription matching the symbols.

Viktor and I walked around and took photos. I translated the Hebrew, Viktor identified the symbols and associated them with the inscriptions. After a few minutes he noticed that the Cohens were buried in the edge plots and asked if there was a reason for it. Once I explained the customs of Cohanim, Viktor made sense of the design and layout of the cemetery and identified its main paths, wide enough and far enough from the other graves so Cohen families could visit the graves of loved ones. The cemetery was pervaded by the same feeling of magic, sanctity and mystery that I'd experienced in a visit to the old Jewish cemetery in Prague. While I pondered these sights, Viktor explained that such cemeteries were found all over Ukraine. "There's barely a city, town, or village without a Jewish cemetery or its remains, whole headstones or their ruins – if you don't see them immediately you can usually look and find some." I had mixed feelings about this: on the one hand it testified to the large communities that once lived here, on the other it was horrific evidence of the lack of any living people, in other words, it was evidence of the scale of extermination. In Ukraine only the dead Jews remain, I couldn't help thinking – at least they escaped the genocide and have a known burial site. I was touched by a simple headstone from 1910. It was less ornate than the others, and the inscription hinted at the tragic end of an old couple: "Here lie husband and wife, who passed away suddenly on the 15th of Shvat in the year 5671 – an old honest man... and an old honest woman..."

Headstone of the old couple
in the Jewish cemetery in Ternopil

After about a five-minute drive we reached the
forest at the outskirts of Ternopil. Viktor stopped
the car by a long narrow monument that glistened
in the sunlight. The monument had inscriptions in
Hebrew, English and Russian. The notable
difference between the Hebrew and the Russian and
English was unexpected. The Hebrew said: "This

place is a mass grave for the righteous who were killed by the Nazis for their devotion to the Lord, may they be damned, the Hashem shall avenge them." The English and Russian versions did not call for vengeance: "In the memory of the holy martyrs Jews that were ruthlessly killed and buried on this side by the Nazis."

When I told Viktor about the difference in phrasing we both hypothesized that the   writers did not want to hurt the locals' feelings. It is well known that a large portion of the extermination of the Jews was carried out by Ukrainians, the local residents. "Everyone here knows Russian, some know English, but no one knows Hebrew," Viktor reasoned, attempting to explain the discrepancy.

I peered into the forest. Apart from dense trees you couldn't tell this forest was different from any other forest I'd ever seen. The trees were the same trees, the path was a regular path, and the ground was covered in dense vegetation. Nature had covered up the atrocities of man. I could not reconcile what I saw with the knowledge that I was standing on the site of a cold-blooded massacre.

We went on driving. Viktor suggested we stop at Husiatyn. "The majority of the town's residents were Jewish up until World War I. They say there's a pretty synagogue; likely in a state of decay, would you like to go see it?" So we drove to Husiatyn. We got directions from some locals, and after a few wrong turns found the synagogue. I stood amazed in front of the deserted building. It was built in a style I did not recognize, a combination of late Renaissance and Moorish influences, probably due to the Turkish occupation. The synagogue was built in the 16th century on the remains of a castle, and was one of the first grand synagogues in Galicia. Its construction began under Turkish rule, but halted when the Turks left by order of the church, to be later renewed under the rule of the Polish nobleman Count Potocki. The Jewish community of Husiatyn flourished until the beginning of World War I, numbering five thousand Jews on the eve of the war, over half the town's population. During the war the Jewish population fled and returned slowly when the war ended. On the eve of World War II the Jewish population numbered some eight thousand people. The Jews of Husiatyn were exterminated as were all the Jews in Galicia, and the grand synagogue stood deserted. Viktor told me the synagogue was barely damaged during World War II, and when the Allies won and Ukraine came under Soviet rule it was turned into a museum. The Soviets continued to maintain the building. They didn't make any architectural changes, so it was easy to identify where the Holy Ark had stood, and above it a relief of the tablets bearing the Ten Commandments. "The museum was shut down when Ukraine became independent, and the building stands deserted, never maintained, crumbling and filthy, as do most of the synagogues in Galicia, and in Chortkow as well," Viktor explained. "It's not a particular slight against the Jews, this is how the government treats most of our heritage – the crumbling castles, and decaying palaces and grand mansions, deserted one after the other. Only the churches are kept in good repair by donations of residents and Ukrainian expats, which is why they look new and thriving."

Husiatyn Synagogue

Only when I saw the grand synagogue, decrepit and in disrepair, through the lens of my camera did I feel emptiness and loss, the feeling that something was missing. What I couldn't feel at the mass grave in Ternopil suddenly hit me in Husiatyn. The disparity between the building's magnificent façade, and the neglect, abandonment and emptiness inside made the absence of Jewish presence palpable. I was ill-at-ease with the realization that only when faced with the physical discrepancy between what is and is not, do I feel the loss.

***

Chortkow

"We're almost in Chortkow, but this isn't the scenic way into town... you won't see the view of the town beneath us because we'll start at the mass grave in the Black Forest." I stood by the monument that was erected by second-generation holocaust survivors living in Israel. I stood and saw how new real-estate developments were closing in on the killing pits. Once again nature was able to cover up the atrocities of man. Once again I could not reconcile what my eyes saw with the knowledge that I was standing in a valley of slaughter – even the monument couldn't evoke that sensation. Only when I noticed two broken old headstones from 1930, which locals had brought to the monument after finding them near their homes, did tears come to my eyes all of a sudden. The ground around the monument was unkempt, weeds grew everywhere and covered up the paving and the open space leading to the road. But the monument stood defiant against the industrial area breathing down its neck, as though saying: we were here first.

Within minutes we were in the city suburbs, by the central bus station; an open space with platforms and stops where men, women with shopping bags, crates, and suitcases stood waiting. A sight that could have been taken directly from Israeli development towns of the 1950s. Viktor turned right and announced that we were arriving at the cemetery. The cemetery was situated on a hill above the town. It took a few moments before I noticed the headstones. At first I saw only a patch of woods and a rusted metal fence encircling the trees. But after Viktor pointed to the woods, I noticed gravestones peeking out among the trees. The 70-year-old-forest had been growing wild in the cemetery since the Jews were exiled and exterminated. It hid the headstones as though concealing them and isolating them from the outside world. Bullets were embedded in some of the headstones, proof of the battles that took place in the graveyard. It was the first time I noticed that the words for grave – kever – and battle – krav – in Hebrew are made up of the same letters. We walked up and down the cemetery, having trouble making our way among the trees, branches, bushes and nettles, taking pictures of headstones so we could later make out names and dates. I searched for relatives, and my grandfather's grave, Isak Finkelman who died in 1933, but in vain. It was clear to me that the forest kept more of the cemetery hidden than visible. Covered in thorns and scratches we left and went on to the center of Chortkow. Viktor stopped at the old Kramer house, my mother's old home. It was afternoon, the city had emptied. I was overwhelmed by the beauty of the old, Austrian-style buildings. Every way I looked I saw evidence of a rich and very different past. Viktor led me to the entrance and rang the doorbell. A woman now living in my family's old home answered the door and Viktor simply explained who I was and asked if she would show me the apartment. Other neighbors joined and quickly volunteered to show me their apartments. "After the war your family's house was divided into smaller apartments. Instead of one apartment per floor, there are two units per floor, some of which are rented out." On the ground floor was commercial space – a large store, and a restaurant. "We'll leave that till tomorrow, when my friend Bogdan will be around and will tell you about the treasure," Viktor quickly explained. The Kramer's apartment was enormous. It matched the detailed description in my mother's memoirs perfectly. It still had the same wood floor, and the current resident laughed when I told how my mother described the way they would polish it. "That's still how it's done today – if you have the strength – strong back and legs," she said. The height of the ceiling was surprising. You could easily build a loft in each apartment. We continued to the third floor. Again the space was huge, and above it, to my surprise, in the attic, one of the tenants built a large pigeon coop with hundreds of carrier pigeons. His home was filled with trophies from many competitions. I smiled when I remembered my mother battling the pigeons that would invade the balcony of our apartment in Haifa. Those pigeon wars were part of my adolescence.

Out in the street again, I noticed for the first time the fishing store at the front of the house. Though my early love of fishing had waned over the years, I never stopped looking at fishing rods and especially fly fishing hooks with their feathers and colorful thread used for catching trout – an aesthetic pleasure I'd never given up. My childhood memory – fishing with my father and his friends – brought tears to my eyes.

I was full to the brim with the day's experiences, and asked Viktor to take a break from the dead and the memories; "Some good pizza and a cold beer after a shower will do the trick. I just can't take any more."

The hotel surprised me – a spacious, modern room; news in Ukrainian coming out of a flat-screen TV, and high speed internet. In just a few minutes, I'll be connected to the world again. I turned on my iPad and tried to slip into another world, but failed – it didn't seem right. Suddenly, I'm alone; sad and shaking like the last leaf on a tree during a storm. Overcome with memories of my family, I fell asleep for a short while. There was excellent pizza in Chortkow. There was delicious cold beer in Chortkow. Viktor and I shared some spicy pizza and cold beer and that was the end of our first evening in Chortkow.

***

Sleeping in Chortkow wasn't easy; waking up was much easier. Despite the comfortable room I had a restless sleep, tossing and turning. I woke up dozens of times, but fell right back to sleep, and when I woke up in the morning I was surprisingly alert and full of energy. We had good coffee at the Italian restaurant in the hotel, and planned our first full day in Chortkow. We both felt that the day before we'd arrived tired and heavy with emotion, and from now on we'd be better off taking it slow and in small doses. We made a list of goals so as not to miss anything... and Viktor read out: "We'll start at the cemetery in the center of town, the one by the Catholic graveyard, we're better off doing that in the morning while it's cool. Afterwards we can go to your father's house at 279 Szpitalna St., which today is called Pihuty St., then we'll continue to the old synagogue next to the medical school and, from there, to the basement of your mother's house to hear the story of the treasure. We'll take a short break at my place for a light lunch – Tania's mother made us borscht – and then go on to meet an historian who runs the local Chortkow museum. He would like to take you on a walking tour. I think this is a good plan. You have plenty of time and there's no need to hurry." I thought it sounded like a plan for a whole week, but decided to go along with Viktor's pace because I had no idea how things might develop.

Within minutes we arrived at our first stop, the Jewish cemetery located by the Catholic cemetery. Viktor explained that it was still in use until the 1930s, when they ran out of space. "The old cemetery was by the hospital, near your father's house, but it was full so they moved here. The old cemetery has only one headstone, that of Rabbi Friedman, Chortkow's rabbi. The other headstones were stolen by the Nazis who used them to pave roads. There are people buried beneath the woods by the hospital, but the graves are no longer marked. We'll go past it later today." We walked around the Catholic cemetery but we couldn't find the Jewish one. When we asked workers digging a new grave where the Jewish graves were they pointed to an area covered in brush at the edge of the cemetery and said, "The Jewish cemetery is covered in trees, you'll have to hop the fence because the gate is locked." After we cleared the stone wall, we saw another tangled thicket and, among the trees, many headstones, some still standing and some in various states of decay. I could not believe my eyes. I knew that the trees had been cut down only five years ago, but the lack of maintenance meant it only encouraged growth. Wherever a trunk had been cut down, four new trunks had grown. In fact, the new trees and the brush protected the graves by preventing people from coming. We walked around methodically as I tried to locate my grandfather's grave, which I hadn't found the day before. On the back of each headstone was the name of the deceased in Polish, which allowed both Viktor and me to search. It felt very strange, like a scene from Indiana Jones: a small dense wood in the center of town... with us chopping branches and making our way from headstone to headstone, trying to find ones that had fallen and were hidden in the brush, or concealed among the trees and bushes. Suddenly I heard Viktor call out, "There's a Finkelman here." Chills ran down my spine as I read the headstone. It was the grave of Eliyahu Finkelman son of Mechel. Eliyahu was my father's cousin. Mechel's father was my grandfather's brother. Eliyahu was my Aunt Zelda's father; he died in 1921 when she was only three, after which she lived in my father's home. Eliyahu is the grandfather of Mordechai and Linette Liebling. It was the only family headstone we found.

I was certain that there were others in the cemetery but they were likely hidden. I stood at the grave of Eliyahu son of Mechel Finkelman and said the Kaddish prayer. It moved me to tears. For over seventy years, and perhaps longer, no one said Kaddish at this grave. It was a prayer for all of my family members whose resting place remained unknown.

Headstone of Eliyahu Finkelman's grave

We left the cemetery full of emotion. Viktor asked about the prayer I'd recited, what language it was in and how long it had existed. I explained its meaning, that it is said in Aramaic and that it predated Christianity.

We were on our way to my father's home when suddenly Viktor stopped the car and pointed to a house on the other side of the road. "That's my house, we'll eat lunch there later, but I just want to show you some headstones right here... let's get out of the car for a few minutes." We stood by a small pile of rubble. I didn't notice the details at first, but after a few seconds I could see it was made up of broken headstones. "These were used for the curb on Pihuty Street. The Nazis used headstones from the old cemetery to pave roads in rural areas, and for curbs in the city." When he saw how appalled I was he explained that in recent years Chortkow has been replacing the curbs and repaving the roads, a slow task that is not yet completed. It was difficult to make out the inscriptions on most of the headstones, but a large piece, weighing close to sixty kilos, was covered in beautiful carvings of a lion holding a crown over the Ark of Torah. The stone was broken on the other side of the crown, where the second lion should have been. I couldn't move. Seeing the fragments of headstones threw me back to my Kaddish prayer earlier. I asked Viktor if we could move the headstone fragment to his place. "I can't bear the thought that it'll just lie here at the side of the road. Let's move it into your garden, where at least its beauty can be appreciated." I don't think he could have refused. He came back with a wheelbarrow and together we managed to place the headstone fragment in his garden.

Headstone fragment that we moved
from the street to Viktor's garden

We drove along Pihuty Street toward the Finkelman house. Of course now I could identify the curb built from headstones and the gaps where they had been removed. I was horrified that this was the road leading to Chortkow's hospital. I immediately recognized the Finkelman home. It was identical to the picture I got from Miri. It was the house that Kobe Kon had described only a few weeks earlier. The house that stood before me was a kind of architectural gem, built by a craftsman in the early twentieth century.

Decorative relief detail on the roof
of the Finkelman home

The house stood at the corner of two streets and was designed with the intersection in mind. At its top was a small lookout tower, decorated with a pretty metal roof, pointing to the sky. The tower was located at the corner facing the intersection and could be seen from a distance. The building style was Austrian with some neoclassical influences and a dash of Viennese art nouveau. I could easily see how my father's interest in architecture began with this house. The inside was simple and pretty with large neat living spaces and a simple, functional design. I told Viktor I'd be glad to take this house back with me to Israel; it was love at first sight. In truth, I was a bit doubtful that this amazing house had been my father's. "Perhaps there was some mistake in the address when the street name was changed, or a mix-up with the house numbers?" I don't know where the feeling came from, but I felt I had to find some proof that this was indeed the right house. I remembered that in my backpack I had, in addition to various documents and old postcards, a photo in which my Aunt Sima, the doctor, was standing outside the family home, and, in the background, you could see a window with decorative trim, the details of which were similar to the decorative elements of this house. I took the photo out and was disappointed; it was similar but not identical. My disappointment was short-lived. "There are windows and decorative trim in the back yard as well," Viktor reported after he walked around the house. The special trim on the back windows was identical to that in the photo. I had no doubt: this house was my father's house.

Dr. Sima Finkelman
in Chortkow

The window trim
in the back yard

The beauty of the house made me forget for a moment the image of the cemetery, the gravestones strewn in the field, and even the road paved from headstones. The aesthetic experience momentarily erased those memories, making way for new experiences later in the day.

We stopped at Viktor's for lunch. This is where I first met Luda, Tania's mother. Luda is a handsome woman, about my age, who lives in Chortkow in a house Viktor is renovating. For many years she lived and worked in Italy. After some time, she obtained Italian citizenship and now splits her time between Italy and Chortkow. Luda made us some delicious borscht. It wasn't like the soup I knew from my childhood. My mother's borscht was cold, sweet and did not contain meat because we ate it with sour cream. Luda's borscht was a hearty meat soup loaded with root vegetables and leafy greens, beets, and potatoes. The soup resembled goulash, but the beets gave it a different flavor and a deep red color. Luda and Viktor thickened their soup with sour cream. I liked the Ukrainian version of borscht and asked Luda for the recipe.

After lunch we went to meet Dr. Jaromir Chorpita, the historian who runs Chortkow's museum. He volunteered to take me on a tour along the Jewish Trail of Chortkow. We walked through many grand houses that used to belong to Jewish families and then down to the ghetto. "The Germans shoved Jews from the richer parts of town into the poor houses along the river. They crammed them into an inhumanly small and crowded space from which it would be hard to escape. It was easy to block off a narrow strip of buildings along the river, because you could not escape in the direction of the river..." When you see the small narrow area of the ghetto with your own eyes, you understand and feel the cramped living conditions and the distress the Jews experienced. It was a veritable death trap. I thought to myself that, unlike the ghettos in the large cities which allowed relatively more movement, the small town ghetto had thousands of people crammed into such a small area that the feelings of desperation and finality were undoubtedly increased. I found it difficult to accept that most of my family had met its end in this place.

From there we continued on foot towards the river. We stood in front of a mostly-empty lot with a small chapel surrounded by a carefully-tended garden. Jaromir said: "Here, in this very place, stood an interesting building which was constructed in the early '30s of the previous century, some ten years before the war. The building's no longer here because it sustained a direct hit in a bombing towards the end of the war and was completely demolished. I wanted to tell you about it because it was different. It was the Jewish Cultural Center. There were also progressive Jews living in Chortkow, and they built a gymnasium for exercise and sports. It was built by a Jewish architect who studied in Vienna..." "Yes, I know," I quickly interposed with a broad grin, "I'm familiar with the story."

Laying the cornerstone for the new Jewish Cultural Center. The stone is being laid by Rabbi Arye Meyer Schechter; Zvi Finkelman handing him the trowel

To their surprise, I asked Viktor to stop translating and give me a moment to show them something I brought with me. Viktor seemed a bit embarrassed as he translated for me. From my backpack, I took out a binder with a page on which I'd photocopied an old photo I'd found in the Chortkow memorial book. The photo showed my father holding a mason's trowel with mortar in the cornerstone ceremony for the new Jewish Cultural Center, the very building that used to stand in the lot in front of us, where we stood in amazement. Jaromir and Viktor just stood there and I started to laugh. It was unbelievable. Of all the gorgeous buildings in town, they take me to see an empty lot where a building used to stand that symbolized a different kind of Jewish culture, a progressive culture, the only building that my father designed and built in Chortkow, a building that was destroyed in the war. All this without having a clue that I was the son of that architect. When Jaromir collected himself he started talking quickly and Viktor had a hard time keeping up: "Our families knew each other well... my grandfather was the train station master and your grandfather had sawmills... my grandfather would let your grandfather know when log shipments were about to arrive so he could plan to unload them from the train cars... All the Finkelmans had sawmills in Jagielnica and Chortkow. The logs arrived from distant places, massive tree trunks. The mills would cut the logs into planks according to the needs of local clients... Your family was the only lumber supplier in the whole town..." I tried to correct him and set things straight to the best of my knowledge, to say that my family were lumber merchants, and that I knew nothing of sawmills. But Jaromir firmly corrected me: "The ground where the Finkelman mills used to stand are still covered in wood chips and sawdust. The layers upon layers of sawdust leave no room for doubt... according to my family's stories, our grandfathers were close friends until your grandfather died in the early '30s... I didn't know your father survived and that you were the grandson... I brought you to the empty lot just so I could tell you that Chortkow was home to many kinds of Jews: Hasidim, Mitnagdim , Maskilim , who unfortunately all shared the same fate... Here you are standing with a photo of the architect and I simply can't believe this is happening..."

Despite having experienced many similar situations regarding my family over the last two years, which I saw as coincidence though incredibly unlikely, I was surprised anew every time. I could never get used to the fact that things take place of their own accord, as if guided by a higher power. This feeling increased when I saw the expressions on the faces of people who were involved, as though they suddenly found themselves in the middle of occurrences for which they did not have any rational explanation, they looked like they'd seen a ghost. So it was with Jaromir as well.

We continued touring the streets of Chortkow for about an hour. We went up to the remains of the castle above the city, we saw the ancient wood churches, but my mind was elsewhere. My thoughts returned to that empty lot where the gymnasium used to be, and the train station where huge logs had been unloaded for my family many years ago. I laughed at my own words said earlier – "today we need to take it slow" – and wondered what else this day might bring.

***

The Treasure

The past burst into the present. We were sitting at a local bar in the basement of my grandfather's house, under a sporting goods and fishing store: Me, Viktor, and Bogdan Mikhailovich, the bar's owner. No, this is not a mistake; there we were at a local bar, in what used to be the basement of my mother's family home. We were sharing a cold one. It felt a bit like a Kaddish prayer. A prayer over beer.

Tears streamed down my face. It's not easy having a drink in my grandfather's basement. This is where the treasure was found. A treasure that grandpa Menachem Mendel Kramer hid before he was kicked out by the Soviets. When Viktor wrote and told me about it, it felt far away, just a story. But here I was. It was electrifyingly real.

Bogdan began telling the story: "They were four downtrodden workers, drunks. They would work till they were spent and once they got their pay they'd buy vodka and go home to Wygnanka to drink. Every day they'd drink their pay away. Gregory Lugofet hired them to dig up the floors and walls. A few weeks earlier he'd come to me with an unusual proposition: 'Since you're not renovating the place, I'll build a restaurant in the cellar under your sporting goods and fishing store. I'll pay for everything, and after two years you'll own it all. In return you won't charge me rent.'"

Bogdan couldn't refuse such an offer. For years the cellar had been used for storage and did not contribute any income. He had started renovating it himself, but didn't have the money to continue the work. Here, suddenly, was an opportunity to complete the renovations and make some money and, on top of that, in the end, he would own a bar. Within days the renovations began.

They dug up the space oddly, as though jumping from one spot to the other. Drilling into the walls then back to jackhammering the floor, and at the end of the day pouring their small wages into a bottle. Bogdan didn't understand their method, but was not worried. The walls were thick and the floor sturdy, so the building's structural integrity was in no danger, and holes could be patched up easily. They knocked down walls and closed up old passageways. The daily banging and clanking reminded Bogdan of a flock of birds pecking at the ground for food. Now and then Lugofet would stop by, tyrannize the workers and move them around, seemingly at random, according to some incomprehensible imaginary plan.

One afternoon, on a day like any other, there was an accident. They'd swung the hammer and broke some rotting wood beams and the floor collapsed, and with it one of the workers. He was quickly pulled out of the wreckage and fortunately wasn't even hurt. But at the end of that workday, in the early evening, they broke their pattern, went into Chortkow and drank away their money right then and there. Drunk and unsteady, they called a cab to take them up the mountain back to Wygnanka. They had always walked. A cab was a luxury. For the price of a cab-ride you could buy a bottle of vodka, the good stuff. They asked the cab driver to load a large trunk into the car and when he refused they tried to convince him in the slurred speech of drunks and tried to bribe him with generous compensation. "We found a treasure, so we can pay you," they went on, and the driver was eventually persuaded for an outrageous price, and drove them home.

As soon as he dropped off the loud, smelly passengers and their strange luggage, the cab driver hurried over to Lugofet's because he felt that he might be rewarded for this kind of information. And so it was. That very evening, after yelling, lengthy arguments and chest thumping and, possibly, even blows, Lugofet offered to buy the trunk from the four workers. Following some loud haggling, the trunk was sold for two thousand dollars per worker. The next day when they threatened to tell the authorities he offered them each another five hundred dollars to keep his secret. It was a large sum of money. Ten thousand dollars was enough to buy a decent house on a nice property, but Lugofet must have known the value of the trunk.

Almost forty years had passed since the last time a treasure was found in Chortkow. At first, in the early years after the war, they would find treasures in the gardens of old Jewish homes, in attics and hidden in the walls. But over the years fewer treasures were discovered. "Even the Jews' money is all gone..."

The rumor spread. It is well known that no one can keep a secret in Chortkow. Within days, the whole town was talking about the treasure. A treasure found sixty four years after the family was exiled from its home.

We were sitting over cold beers in the bar in my grandfather's house. My throat was dry and tight, and my salty tears mixed with the bitter beer. Bogdan continued to tell his story and I listened in silence. "Everyone knew the treasure contained large icons and pieces of pure silver. Rumor had it that a safe was found in the wall and it contained gold and silver coins... it was a real treasure.

When I asked for my share, as the owner of the place where the treasure was found, Lugofet insisted that it was not part of our deal." When the rumors reached the police, Bogdan, as the owner, was brought in for questioning but quickly released. Later, Lugofet's son was arrested. He disappeared for a week then was released and was gone, probably after having given the investigators what they wanted. Eventually, it turned out he'd immigrated to the US.

After a few weeks Lugofet bought a large piece of land and built a grand house. A few months later he bought a café, and sent his son to live in the US. "as everyone in Ukraine knows, that too requires a lot of money." In time, Lugofet left the renovated basement as promised. The four workers drank away their money. They improved their accommodations, but quickly went back to work as casual laborers and did not significantly improve their lives. In fact, anyone who had a hand in the treasure suffered some misfortune. Lugofet divorced three times, knew no peace of mind, and, according to the locals became very eccentric. One worker disappeared, supposedly due to illness. Another died shortly after the treasure was discovered. A third worker has terminal cancer, and the fourth is probably abroad, his whereabouts unknown, he might have died, even his family lost track of him.

That night I couldn't sleep. I was restless. Something in the story didn't fit. Something was wrong, or not quite accurate. In those restless hours I kept going over the story. I read my notes over and over again. Finally I fell asleep, likely shortly before dawn, and woke up excited with a new insight: Jewish families don't keep icons of saints... it must have been Jewish ritual objects, ornaments of the Torah and holy vessels from the Stratyn Kloyz. Grandfather must have hidden items from the synagogue in a trunk he buried in the cellar, and his own money and property in a safe in the wall. I understood then that my grandfather had prepared for the Soviet invasion. He knew his property would be taken and he would be ostracized for being wealthy, as the Soviets did in all the lands under their rule. He knew that the synagogue would be shut down and that prayer and worship would be banned. I had not the slightest doubt that these were the facts; it explained why the treasure was so great – worth about five hundred thousand dollars, according to Chortkow rumor.

Grandfather was the beadle of the Hasidic Stratyn Kloyz, together with Pinchas Shifris, Miri Gershoni's grandfather. They weren't neighbors, but like many others in Chortkow, were connected through their adherence to the Stratyn Hasidic movement. It was a rich community, and as beadles they were responsible for the kloyz property, as well as the property of the Hasidic movement and the community. They must have been able to hide the treasure after the Soviets had already arrived. They did such a good job that the treasure wasn't found. I assume my family used up some of the coins and silver in order to survive, build hiding places, "bunkers", and dig escape tunnels. They prepared all that in advance. They would have needed people to share their secret, I thought, maybe locals, Poles or Ukrainians. Perhaps Lugofet is the descendent of one of those people, or the grandson of a cook or other employee who worked in the house. He might have bought the information. But one thing was certain: he had made the deal with the express purpose of digging and finding the treasure.

My grandfather's family may have used up part of the treasure, but they would not have touched the sacred ceremonial objects. Those would be safeguarded for better days, and when the situation never got better and the beadles were murdered, the treasure was forgotten, like many other treasures in Chortkow.

By the next day everyone in Chortkow knew I was there: The grandson of the man who hid the treasure under Bogdan's sporting goods shop. After all, rumors spread fast in Chortkow...

That evening I was invited for perogies at my grandfather's house, at the bar where the treasure was found. It was an encounter with a taste of childhood from my mother's kitchen. There are certain childhood flavors that you never forget... the dumplings were moon-shaped, filled with mashed potatoes and fried onion and served with fresh sour cream like they used to be served in the days when no one counted calories or cared about fat content. We sat there, Viktor and Bogdan and I, and shared hot perogies and cold beer.

"Don't go near Lugofet," Bogdan warned me "he's unpredictable, a bit crazy and aggressive. But one of the workers who found the treasure still lives in Wygnanka. He's very sick, he has cancer, but you could try, he might be willing to talk. His name is Tolik." Viktor was surprised "That's the second husband of my brother-in-law's first wife. She's Jewish. Her name is Raya, let's set up a meeting."

The next day we met with Raya Yakir, wife of Tolik, the worker with cancer. When I introduced myself as an Israeli visiting his parents' old homes and started telling of my father's house on Szpitalna Street she stopped me and said: "Let's talk about the basement under the sporting goods shop, that too used to belong to your family..." They were right, I thought, word travels quickly in Chortkow. Raya, who was expecting my visit, verified the story of the treasure.

***

No more surprises, I thought. After hearing Bogdan's story of the treasure. I remembered thinking that morning, "you need to take things slowly today... in small doses." But clearly events in Chortkow have their own dynamics. Viktor, who saw I was exhausted, took me back to the hotel, gave me two hours to shower, rest, and buy some cold beer, and invited me to a barbeque in his back yard. "Luda and Tania, who's now in Chortkow, will take care of most of it, you just relax and enjoy and I'll cook the meat." "Sounds like an excellent plan," I replied with a smile, "I could do with meat and beer on a chilly Chortkow evening such as this."

A cool twilight descended. Viktor was in charge of grilling the meat. Large skewers of superb meat with fresh vegetables from the garden. A wonderful meal. I felt relaxed, the day's events slowly sinking into the background, making way for light conversation about life in Ireland, Italy and Israel. How similar people's basic pleasures are; a different country, different culture, different history, but the food and beer, the stars above and the rituals of barbequing make us all feel good. We sat and talked, ate and drank, and drank, and drank until the moment when Tania handed me an envelope. "These are the documents I brought from the archive. Sorry I didn't give them to you sooner."

I've seen all kinds of shipping documents in my life: documents for shipping merchandise, confirmation for registered mail, invoices for shipping by air, sea and land, but I never thought I'd see "shipping documents" sending people to their death. I froze in my seat when Viktor translated: "The date is November 19, 1942, this is a list of those sent from the Ternopil Central train station to be relocated in Belzec. Your aunt, Dr. Sima Finkelman, is on line 12 and her number is Rp 7-159."

Obviously this dose of information was too much for me, totally out of proportion, unacceptably huge. I lay in bed in the hotel, my eyes wide open staring at the ceiling, making a mental list and enumerating:

looking for family graves in the cemetery and saying Kaddish over the grave of Mordechai and Linette's grandfather, Zelda's father; finding the broken headstones from Szkolna Street and moving one to Viktor's garden; visiting the Finkelman home; touring the city with Dr. Jaromir Chorpita and unwittingly being led to the spot where the Jewish Cultural Center designed by my father once stood; the story of the Kramer treasure; and finally the shipping documents sending my Aunt Sima to her death. Six events that had shaken me such that my eyes simply would not shut.

Document "relocating" Dr. Sima Finkelman (marked
with the arrow) to the Belzec extermination camp

***

Kaddish

For two days we travelled in south-western Ukraine, in Galicia towns that had a rich history of Jewish communities. We visited amazing castles, ancient fortresses and keeps; among them the wonderful castle in the city of Kamianets-Podilskyi and the Khotyn Fortress on the banks of the Dniester River. We visited Chernivtsi (Chernovich) in the Bukovina region and Buchach, hometown of the author S.Y. Agnon, Jagielnica, neighboring town of Chortkow from which the Finkelmans came, and Yazlovets from which the Kramer family came. Pepe Kramer, who lived in the family home and was a friend of my uncle Moshe and Tonia Sternberg, was probably also from Yazlovets.

I felt I had to leave Chortkow and visit other places to give myself a break. I wanted to clear my head of all the emotional upheavals I had been through in such a short time. Despite my wish to distance myself from the "Jewish experience" even for a few hours, I was unable to. Every place, every village, carries with it Jewish history from both the ancient and recent past: an old synagogue, a cemetery, headstones strewn in a field – all testimony of the magnificent Jewish community that once lived there. So we found ourselves, Tania, Viktor, and me, looking for synagogues in villages and towns, and old cemeteries and broken headstones at the side of the road and in pastures among hefty Ukrainian cows. There was something pretty, out of context, in the contrast between the broken gravestones and the wide open fields, that created a different kind of aesthetic experience which was enjoyable in and of itself.

Only once I was home, and shared my experiences, did Raya, my wife, provide the feedback and insight that made the connection between the castles, the fields of headstones and the cemeteries: "The old castles and fortresses are also a kind of monument to a life and culture that have passed from this world." That sentence was enough to summarize my visit to the towns and villages of south western Ukraine. Evidence of the grandeur of the past compared with the dilapidation of the present stood out everywhere, proof of a culture that had disappeared and will never return.

We drove to Chernivtsi. Viktor wanted me to see a beautiful city that has been preserved and has survived the slings and arrows of history.

For some reason, I thought Chernivtsi was in the Bukovina region in Romania. Viktor corrected me – this seemed to be a common misconception.

Bukovina was a duchy and region in the Austro-Hungarian Empire and, after WWI was part of Romania. After WWII the southern half of Bukovina remained within Romanian borders, but its northern half, including the city of Chernivtsi, became part of Ukraine.

We left early in the morning; the drive took about an hour and a half. The light traffic made maneuvering between the many potholes easier. When we arrived in Chernivtsi, Viktor stopped the car in front of a large neoclassical building typical of the early twentieth century. "This is the Chernivtsi train station. The road we came by would have been the escape route your parents and sister took when the war broke out... they would have arrived here by train and continued in horse-drawn carriages because the tracks were bombed. It was indeed, like you told me, the last train on which the Polish government fled to Romania..."

A number of times during our drive, when I saw the train tracks winding alongside the road I considered it might have been my parents' escape route, because the general direction was south, towards Romania. But despite those earlier thoughts, I was taken by surprise. Again I felt the familiar feeling of the last few days, that my route in Ukraine was predetermined, and that somehow I had been led along the tracks of my family's fate.

Chernivtsi train station

Chernivtsi's beauty took my breath away. Not for nothing is it known as "Little Vienna". Many houses in the center of town are fine examples of the architecture that was typical of the period of the Austro-Hungarian Empire. The theater, built in 1905, and the university campus, built in 1882, are perfect examples of the beauty of that culture. The Jewish Cultural Center, in the theater plaza, surprised me in its size and beauty, evidence of the size of the Jewish community on the eve of WWII. It is a shame that the central synagogue built in 1873,

and one of the grandest in Europe, was burned by
the Germans in 1941. Later, during the Soviet period,
the building's interior was destroyed, but its façade
was preserved and it was converted in 1959 to a
cinema. The building, designed in the Neo-Moorish
style, exhibits North African and Spanish influences,
which were seen as exotic and were a part of the
culture in that period, the same influences that I had
seen in many other, smaller-scale buildings in
Chortkow. The visit to Chernivtsi was like a breath
of fresh air, an aesthetic experience of manicured
streets and wonderful architecture. So I was not
surprised to discover a few buildings in the Art
Nouveau and Art Deco styles, because, without a
doubt, the Chernivtsi of the past was a rich city with
a grand culture.

We walked about town and eventually reached the
Jewish Quarter, which is still referred to as the Shtetl
today, and, to my surprise, found an active
synagogue. I seized the opportunity and went in
with Tania and Viktor. After getting permission
from the beadle, I opened the Ark of the Torah and
showed Viktor and Tania the handwritten Torah
scroll and the ornaments that were in the ark with
it, explaining that these were likely the kind of
objects found in the treasure trunk in my
grandfather's house. It was Viktor and Tania's first

visit to an active synagogue, rather than one that is ruined, neglected, or used as a library or warehouse.

Even the Jewish cemetery in Chernivtsi was unusually large and beautiful. The Christian and the Jewish cemeteries are across the street from each other. The Jewish cemetery is larger, with more than fifty thousand people buried there. Its grounds and size, as well as the beauty of the large cleansing room, were evidence of the grand and rich history of the Jewish community in Chernivtsi before the Holocaust. I could see that it was still active to some extent, and, like the synagogue, was further evidence that a small Jewish community still existed in the city.

The drive back to Chortkow was relaxed and uneventful. I dozed off for much of it, my thoughts drifting from pretty houses to gravestones, past to present. As we entered Chortkow, Viktor offered to take me back to the hotel for a short rest. I thought it sounded strange because I'd invited them to join me that evening for a dinner of pizza, beer, and wine at the Italian restaurant in the hotel, so the schedule didn't seem to make much sense. I sensed something wasn't right, and when I asked directly why we needed a break I received a surprising response: "It's been 60 days, today, since our baby died. Customarily we visit the grave after 30 days, 60 days, and a year, so we need a break." Without hesitating I said I'd be happy to join the memorial... after days of such intense shared emotions the separation seemed unnatural.

We drove to Wygnanka. In an open field covered in flowers, in a well-tended cemetery under a clear blue sky and a setting sun, we stood, Tania, Viktor, and I, by a small earth mound covered in dozens of white flowers and baby toys, and said not a word. Silence hung heavy, Tania cried softly, Viktor didn't move. I could hear him breathing over the weeping and the birds chirping.

"Would you like me to say Kaddish?" I asked when I realized there wasn't any ceremony or prayer. "Of course," they responded immediately. And so I found myself standing by a baby's grave, under the Chortkow sky, the setting sun washing the sky red, and saying Kaddish for a baby I never knew.

The words stuck in my throat. Overcome with tears, I suddenly felt the magnitude of the contrast, the absurdity or, perhaps more, the significance of the moment: that I, Yaron – a Jew whose parents were from Chortkow and whose families were murdered in the Holocaust; son of a people that mourned hundreds of thousands of babies murdered in infinite cruelty and whose burial place remained unknown, among whom was Lijuchnia who appears in my Aunt Zelda's diary – am standing here saying Kaddish for a baby of Christian parents on Chortkow ground. I stood with them and cried.

Kaddish

May His great name be magnified and sanctified
In the universe that was created according to His will
And may His Kingdom be established
And may redemption sprout forth
And may His anointed one come.

May it happen in your lifetime
And in your days
And in the lifetime of all the House of Israel
Speedily and very soon
And they should say "*Amen*"

May His great name be blessed forever and ever and ever

May the name of the Holy One, blessed be He,
be blessed and lauded and beautified
and exalted and raised up and glorified
and elevated and praised

Higher than any blessing and song,
praise and consolation
that we could say in the world

And they should say *Amen*

In Hebrew, I prayed this prayer

***

The Myth

How strange it is to be introduced to a story that every child in Chortkow knows; be it myth or legend, it is the story of the origin of the name Chortkow.

The story, rooted in Slavic mythology, revolves around the eternal battle between good and evil, God and the Devil. God builds and creates, and the Devil (Chort in Polish) ruins and destroys, constantly interfering with God's plans. Local legend tells that when God created the Seret River, which runs through Chortkow, the Devil tried with all his might to stop its flow. God and the river fought the Devil. The Devil failed, and, as he was struggling with God, fell into the river, got tangled in the reeds (ocheret) and drowned. There he remains, according to the legend, trapped among the reeds at the bottom of the river. That is why the valley around the river is named Chortkova Dolyna – The Devil's Valley. The Chortkowskyi family is named after the valley where they lived, and the town in the middle of the valley – Chortkow – is named after the family. The Chortkowskyi family built the first wooden church in Chortkow in the 16th century. Viktor and Bogdan told me that some of the locals, Bogdan among them, organized and tried to change the town's unusual name more than once. They circulated petitions, but couldn't get the name changed. Time after time they ran into obstacles.

When I heard the story the first thoughts to cross my mind were: How come I've never heard this story before? How come the legend wasn't told or mentioned in the literature written about Chortkow? Why was the eternal battle between good and evil missing from Chortkow's Jewish folklore? And, given the terrible tragedy that was the extermination of all the Jews in this town and region, a town where every third resident was wiped off the earth, how did the Jews never mention the diabolical fate that was hinted at in the town's name or the battle of good and evil. I had many questions, but not even a sliver of an answer. My mother used to say, "Chortkow was a kind of paradise until, one day, it changed completely and turned into hell."

From the moment I heard the legend, the story of Chort, son of the Slavic god Chernobog and the goddess Mara, became part of the metaphysical explanation for the fate of Chortkow's Jews, and the fate of my family. The Jewish residents of Chortkow, like many Jews in Galicia, studied Kabbalah and understood the meaning of words and names and their power over people's destiny. Some even changed their first or last name as a way to solve problems of health or income. How could they not understand the hidden message in the name of the place where they lived? How could they ignore the warning signs and go on with their lives in the Devil's Valley as though tomorrow could bring nothing but good fortune. The extermination of Chortkow's Jews was unprecedented. To my knowledge, it was more thorough than the extermination of Jews in any other region. Only 80 people from Chortkow survived, less than one percent (0.8%) of the Jewish population on the eve of the war. For comparison, in Poland, Europe's chief valley of slaughter, twelve percent of the Jewish population survived, of which seven percent fled to the USSR. In Chortkow's neighboring provinces about ten percent of the Jewish population survived, the great majority having fled east and south when the war began. I thought that, if there was no rational explanation for such a thorough extermination, then perhaps the metaphysical interpretation I found could have, at least, foretold that my family was doomed. Was it coincidence that Tonia's brother was murdered on the river? Was it sheer chance that my mother's family's bunker was flooded with water from the river and her whole family drowned? Or, was it chance that brought me, after an eighteen-month-long unexpected journey, tracing my family's past, to Chortkow to sit with Viktor and Bogdan, on a pleasant evening after a hot day, to hear a legend about the origin of the evil that resides within the river. The evil that one day rose and turned heaven to hell, as my mother had said. It raged, killed, murdered, abused and wiped out so many innocent people, including my family.

Over a cold beer in a local bar I learned what many did not know, refused to hear, hid or erased from their memory of the place: the devil, who so efficiently erased the memory of Mordechai Liebman and many like him, had always been there. For an instant, I thought the valley expanded, the river flooded and evil continued its everlasting battle with God...

Chortkow is a beautiful place situated in a verdant valley through which a river flows.

Chortkow Valley – Chortova Dolyna

***

Epilogue

This book was published in Hebrew on May 3rd, 2014.

On May 23rd, at 1 a.m., I received the following email:

Dear Yaron,

My name is Nelly Segal. I found your email address in some correspondence with the wonderful Miri Gershoni.

I live in New Jersey and just arrived in Israel for a visit the other day, and, today, Nurit Yosefi brought me your book about your family and its Chortkow roots.

I started reading it this evening, still struggling with jetlag, when suddenly there popped up the name of Mordechai Liebman, who was my mother's close friend during her youth in Chortkow, a very special, beloved person in my childhood who used to write to me from Egypt, where he was stationed by the British Army. Not merely tales of this-and-that, but actual stories, accompanied by sketches, of colorful characters, members of the Allied Forces, with whom he served during World War II.

After the war he married Sima (yes, same name as your aunt), who was also enlisted and whom he'd met during their military service.

They used to visit us quite often in our home in Beit Oved and we used to visit them, they lived in a house with a garden at the edge of Hadar neighborhood, at the bottom of Mt. Carmel, just above Hillel Street as best as I recall. But if I'm not mistaken they – or maybe just Mordechai (whom we called Mucho) – used to live on Hillel street.

If you'd like any additional bits and pieces of memories, don't hesitate to call me. Looking at the time, I see it's already tomorrow, and in order to function properly, I'd better get some sleep...

In the meantime, all the best,

Nelly

And so, to my utter amazement, the characters in the book continued to emend the facts.

That same night, I called Nelly and learned that Mordechai had Hebraicized his last name. Obviously, after such a dramatic development, I couldn't sleep, so I used the rest of the night to track down Mordechai's past.

Within a few hours, I found in the British Mandate's records that Mordechai's name had originally been Marcus Liebman, and in 1939 he'd changed it to Mordechai Lev-Man. The full picture immediately became clear: Mordechai Liebman, my father's co-owner of the lot, was never officially known by that name; he went by the name Marcus Liebman or Mordechai Lev-Man, which is why I hadn't been able to locate him. The fact that his photo appears on the Meiselman family's memorial page on the Chortkow website also made sense now; Mordechai, who was indeed Shmuel Meiselman's friend from Chortkow and my father's friend in Betar, had served in the British army alongside Asher Meiselman. So, his photo was erroneously added to the memorial page, next to the photos of the Meiselman family.

The next day I managed to discover that Mordechai had a brother, Haim, and a sister, Yona, who immigrated to Israel with their mother, Tzilla. Mordechai's father, Ben Zion, died in Chortkow. Mordechai and Sima had no children. Mordechai was killed in a car accident in 1961, at the age of 50.

Within a few days, I tracked down Mordechai's family and met his two nieces: Ilana, Haim's daughter, and Esther, Yona's daughter. They told me that Mordechai had studied architecture at the

Technion and was employed by the City of Haifa, as an architect.

Every year on the 10th of Tevet, my father's yahrzeit, I'd linger at my father's grave, wondering at the simple elegance of his headstone. When I asked, "How come Dad has such a beautiful headstone?", my mother used to reply: "It was made by your father's good friend, who was an architect for the City of Haifa ..."

Strangely enough, she never mentioned his name.

About Writing

When writing this book I was describing the developments as they took place, almost in real time. It served as a diary while my personal journey unfolded over some 26 months.

I would like to stress that at any given point the writing describes, or is based upon, the knowledge available to me at the time. As my personal journey progressed, and the story with it, new information was added. I chose not to go back and change the story according to new information I discovered. For this reason the reader may find some inaccuracies or contradictions between earlier chapters and information revealed later on.

Perhaps the book should have been edited differently, and my Aunt Zelda Finkelman-Liebling's diary, as well as Jan Kruczkowski's testimony should have been moved to the end. But I felt that both chapters were important in the way they contributed to my ability to better understand and feel the events that took place in Chortkow during the war. Both chapters played a key role in my growing desire to visit Chortkow, experience it and get to know it.

For the reader's convenience I have added a list of names of family members mentioned in the book, and their relation to me, as well as a family tree.

Family members:

The Kramer family, my mother's family:

Menachem Mendel, my grandfather – murdered in the Holocaust 1890-1942

Fradel, my grandmother – murdered in the Holocaust 1888-1942

Malca (Malia), my mother 1911-2013

Anshel, my uncle – murdered in the Holocaust 1917-1942

Selka, my aunt – murdered in the Holocaust 1920-1942

Moshe, my uncle – murdered in the Holocaust 1922-1942

Pepe, second cousin – murdered in the Holocaust 1922-1942

The Finkelman family, my father's family:

Isak, Itzig, my grandfather 1868-1933

Rivka, my grandmother – murdered in the Holocaust 1870-1942

Ethel, my aunt – immigrated to the US 1889-1958

Chaskel, my uncle – immigrated to Colombia 1890-1971

Zelda, my aunt – survived and immigrated to Colombia 1891-1965

Zigush, cousin – survived and immigrated to Colombia 1929

Dr. Sima, my aunt – murdered in the Holocaust 1899-1942

Shlomo Zvi, my father 1908-1958

Zanka, second cousin (my mother's classmate) – murdered in the Holocaust 1911-1943

Lijuchnia, Zanka's baby – murdered in the Holocaust 1940-1943

Hudel, second cousin – murdered in the Holocaust 1915-1942

Zelda (Liebling), second cousin – survived and immigrated to the US 1918-1998

Eliyahu (Loushu), second cousin – survived and immigrated to Israel   1923-2002

The Finkelmans, my father's family

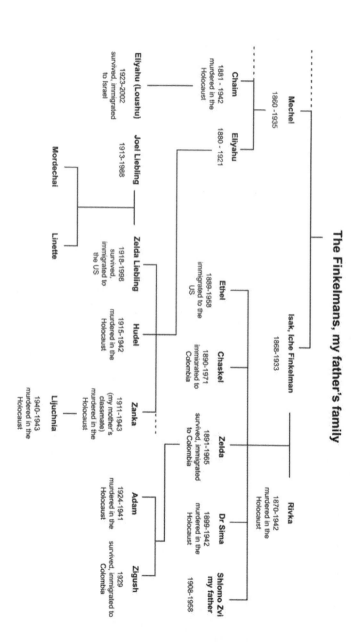

The Kramers, my mother's family

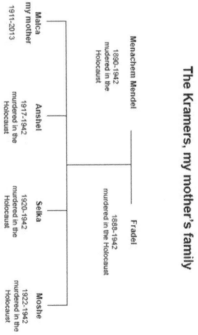

Menachem Mendel
1890-1942
murdered in the Holocaust

Fradel
1888-1942
murdered in the Holocaust

Malca
my mother
1911-2013

Anshel
1917-1942
murdered in the Holocaust

Seika
1920-1942
murdered in the Holocaust

Moshe
1922-1942
murdered in the Holocaust

Second cousin:

Pepe
1922-1942
murdered in the Holocaust

Acknowledgements

My encounter with Israeli bureaucracy began the moment Attorney-at-Law Elinor Kroitoru, head of Location & Information at Hashava, The Company for Location and Restitution of Holocaust Victims' Assets, contacted my family. It continued through the connection I made with Hanni Amor, at the Custodian General's bureau of the Ministry of Justice, and ended with receiving compensation equal to the lot's worth from the Israel Land Administration. My encounter with the Israeli establishment was a positive one, to say the least. I would like to thank all the public servants involved for their dedication and empathy, throughout my quest to locate the lot and have it returned.

I would like to thank Ms. Ada Sales of the Technion in Haifa for searching the Technion archives and finding my father's student file from 1932. Without that file I would not have been able to solve the puzzle.

A special thanks to Miri Gershoni for opening a window to a world I didn't know, and infecting me with the "Chortkow bug", for helping me uncover invaluable information about my family, and for her encouragement during this journey.

Marta Goren's book Voices from the Black Forest was of great service to me while writing. Her book provided me with accurate details of Chortkow's tragic history during World War II.

Thank you to Hanna Avni for sharing with me your mother's, Tonia Vermuth testimony about her own fate as well as the fate that befell my mother's family in the Holocaust.

Warmest thanks to Viktor and his family, my partners in my journey in Chortkow, for arranging the trip, for their generous hospitality, for their superb tour-guiding, locating information and setting up meetings with local residents.

A special thank you to Hanan Schaham, my associate, for listening, for his advice and for encouraging me to put pen to paper and document these events. Also thank you to his wife, Idith, for her legal counsel.

A heartfelt thank you to my editor, Simona Hanoch, for her sensitivity, gentleness and professionalism which greatly helped bring together this final product.

Thank you to Lee Oshrat for the cover design.

Thank you to my translation & editing team, Nina Davis and Shira Davis, for their accurate yet lively translation that captures my voice and style.

Thank you to my friend Camilla Conlon for proofreading.

Thank you to my sister, Ilana, for urging me to write down the story so it will not be forgotten.

Thank you to my wife, Raya, for her insights and unfailing support along this journey.

I am convinced that without the considerable help I received from these people, and others, the journey would not have taken place and the story would not be told. For that I am eternally grateful.

Made in the USA
Middletown, DE
05 December 2017